How to Make a Million Dollars

Brian Teasley
HowToMakeaMillion.com

Legal Disclaimer - Note to Readers

This publication contains ideas and opinions of the author. It is meant to be entertaining, informative, and helpful, but the strategies and processes discussed herein may not be suitable for all people. The strategies and processes discussed are not warranted or guaranteed to produce any specific result.

This book does not provide any personalized legal, financial, accounting, or investment advice. Readers are advised to contact professionals in these topics before proceeding with any actions.

The author and publisher specifically disclaim any liability, loss, or risk which is incurred as a consequence, directly or indirectly, of the use and/or application of any of the contents of this work.

For anyone who has the American entrepreneurial spirit….

"I made a million dollars. I'll show you how I did it, so you can, too."

-Brian Teasley

Contents

The Kid in the Parking Lot

———————◆———————

As I parked my car, a 25-year-old kid pushed a line of carts through the grocery store's parking lot. He saw my car and ran to it. He asked me, "What do you do?" I smiled. "It doesn't matter what I do," I told him. "What matters is you—what you know and what you are going to do."

I have grown accustomed to questions like this. After I earned my million dollars, I bought a car. A beautiful car. The second most beautiful car in the history of the world. It is an AMG SLS coupe. It is scary fast and the classic silver exterior with red interior version looks strikingly beautiful. It also attracts quite a bit of attention.

People are welcome to take photos and videos of it, and they often do. However, I like it when I get the "What do you do?" question. It is always from a man, and he is always around the age of twenty-five. The question is not really "What do you do?" The question he is really asking is, "How do I get a car like this?"

This is a very good question to ask. The questions you ask yourself are very, very important, as we will see later in this book. Whenever someone asks this question, I take the time to answer carefully. My hope is that they are inspired to take the action required to change their life forever in a positive way. So, I gave him a bit more in-depth answer.

"There's a book. I read the book, did what it says, and now you see this car. It's that easy..." I told him.

"But what do you do?" he asked again, a bit confused this time.

"It's not about what I do. It's about what *you* know and do."

"I don't know anything," he said.

"Sure you do," I countered. "Look, this might sound funny, but you know way more about grocery carts than I do. Every day you are out here pushing them, right?"

"Yes," he agreed.

"So, let's say you come up with a device that makes a cart better somehow. I have no idea what that might be. Maybe it straps a child in and makes him safer. Maybe it makes the cart roll better or allows more groceries to fit into the cart. I have no idea what the improvement is. The point is that *you* are much more likely to come up with that idea than I am, because of your experience here every day."

"Okay, so?" he asked.

"Well, let's say you can make the device and sell it to the store for a simple one-dollar-per-cart profit. How many carts do they have here?" I asked.

"About 300," he said.

"Ok, that means you just made $300," I responded. "Now, how many stores do they have in this area?"

"I don't know, around ten I guess."

"Ok, so you just made $3,000. How many other states is this chain in?" I asked.

"A total of... eight," he answered.

"See, you know plenty of things I don't know. My math says you just made $24,000 for your device. What about competitors across the country? How many similar chains are there? At least ten?"

"Sure, probably," he answered

"Ok, that gives you $240,000. With that, you have the car and plenty of money left over for gas. All because you had one simple idea on how to improve a grocery cart."

I could see the wheels spinning in his brain. I love seeing that. I could tell he got it. I told him the name of the book and went on my way. That is the best I can do for someone. I can give them the road map, explain that it is about them and is all up to them... and then... well, then it is all up to them.

In this case, "them" is *you*. It is all up to you. You want to make a million dollars? I am going to show you what to do. Step-by-step, I will tell you exactly how I did it, and in the process, you will figure out how *you* are going to do it.

The ideas you will come up with will be unique and appropriate for *you*. *You* will be the perfect person to think of, develop, and execute your million-dollar idea(s).

Are you ready? Let's get started.

Desire

The day I changed my thinking from "I should do something" to "I must do something," good things started to happen. My level of desire changed from indifferent to sufficient. This led me to invent the world's first handheld GPS tour guide system and ultimately to a million dollars.

When I had this change in attitude, I lived in New York City. I did data analysis and everything was fine. I lived in the greatest city in the world. I paid my rent every month and even saved some money. However, it did not seem like it was enough to ensure a rock-solid, secure future. Even though I loved working on my own compared to working in the same office building every day, it felt like I needed to do more... and something different.

"What could I do to make a *lot* of money?" I wondered. I did not have the answer. I knew I wanted to. I thought I might be ready. But I did not know how to do it. "I know what I'll do—I'll ask for advice from some guys that already make a lot of money!" I decided.

I was already part of an online marketing group that shared ideas and information. Some of the guys in the group were making millions per year helping people with their marketing. These were the people from who I wanted to get advice—people that were very successful at what they were doing.

So, I asked the group, "If you were to recommend to me one business book I should read, what would it be?" I quickly received several answers. To my surprise, four of the guys recommended the same book. That was enough direction for me. I was certainly going to read it. Then I received a second surprise. This book was not new—it was eighty years old!

I hesitated. An eighty-year-old book? I did not want to read an eighty-year-old business book. How could it be relevant to today? However, since I had sought advice from these guys, and so many suggested the same book, I went ahead and bought a used copy of it for six dollars. I am glad I did. I read the book, did what it said, and now I am a millionaire.

What is Your Level of Desire?

The purpose of the story is to alert you to the importance of your level of desire. As soon as I changed my desire level from "I should" to "I must," everything changed. I took the first step (asking for help and recommendations), which lead to the second (buying the book), and so on. I sought advice from a *good* source. I acted on the advice I received and bought the book. Then I read it. Excited by the book, I had no problem doing what it instructed. My desire to improve, my desire to make something happen, my desire to do something new—were so strong that it propelled me forward. All of this happened after my thinking changed from "I should do something" to "I must do something."

You are reading this book. That is a good sign. It shows you are willing to take steps towards your million dollars. If you follow the instructions in this book, that is another good sign, as you will be on your way to your money.

If your level of desire is at "I should do something," you must change it to "I must do something." You have to *believe* you must do something. You have to *feel* you must do something. Simply, you *must* do something. Nothing will change in your life if you do not *do* something. If you go to your job every day and are not doing something that might make you a million dollars, then you are never going to have a million dollars.

If you do not feel you an urgency that you *must* do something, then do not waste your time trying. Your internal flame of desire must be strong enough that when winds blow against it, it stays lit. If your desire level is too low, you will blow out at the first sign of adversity.

An Example

One day in New York City, I had an amusing conversation during an elevator ride in my apartment building. The two girls taking the ride down with me had started a high-end apparel business about three months earlier. They used money from their parents to start the business and pay the rent for their apartment.

"How is your business going? How are sales?" I asked them. In an unconcerned manner one of them answered, "Oh, we are not worried about that. We have a five-year plan."

I knew immediately that their business would fail. Their level of concern and their level of desire simply did not match what is needed to start a business and make it succeed. These two girls liked being able to say, "We are starting a fashion business." But they did not have the necessary level of desire to actually make it work. Sure enough, their store soon vanished, and they were out of their apartment by the end of the year.

Their level of desire contrasted sharply with the desire I had for my New York City handheld GPS tour guide project. The project excited me, and I had a large desire to make it work and earn a large sum of money from it. I enjoyed working with the technology, and I enjoyed studying the original military specifications of the United States Global Positioning Satellite system. I enjoyed meeting people in a local Starbucks when I searched for someone to speak Italian, French, Spanish, and German for the Rockefeller Center version of the system. My desire to make the system work, coupled with my enjoyment of the work, enabled me to do everything necessary to succeed.

You need the same thing. You need a high level of desire. You need to work on something that you enjoy or are interested in. The strong desire to succeed plus enjoying the work will propel you through the hard work it might take to reach your goals. If things get difficult, if some aspects of your project "don't work," then your high level of desire will see you through those times.

Action Required

Think for a moment to determine your passions. Ask yourself: What is your desire? What do you like, enjoy, love? How do you incorporate this into your million-dollar idea? Do not worry if the answers do not come to you right now while reading these words. For now, we are just planting seeds.

To make your million dollars you *must* take action. If you are living and working day-to-day, you must change. You must find time to find your million-dollar idea. Then you must find time to execute your idea and bring it to the world. But first, your level of desire must be strong enough—so strong that your feeling changes from "I should do something to make a million dollars" to "I *must* do something to make a million dollars."

How Strong Does It Need to Be?

In 2000, an eleven-year-old girl's parents asked what she wanted to do on her summer vacation. Unlike many young girls, she did not tell her parents she wanted to go to Disneyland or go to the beach. She wanted and desired to be a singer. So, she told her parents she wanted to go to Nashville, Tennessee—the home of country music.

Her parents took her to Nashville. They visited the offices of music companies and gave them a CD with her music on it. Was she instantly hired as new talent? No. They politely rejected her. They told her, "No."

The land of music, Nashville had just told her, "No, thank you." Did this end her dream of being a singer? No, her desire was too strong.

Instead of accepting defeat, she badgered her parents to move from Pennsylvania to Nashville. When the girl was just thirteen, she somehow managed to convince her parents to move the six hundred miles. Once she was living in Nashville, she got an after-school job with Sony Music. She took vocal lessons and wrote songs. Three years later, she released an album called "Taylor Swift." Fifteen years after she released her first album, her net worth was over $400,000,000.

Taylor Swift's desire was so strong that at age thirteen she was able to convince her parents to leave their home and move hundreds of miles. The good news is that to make your million your desire does not have to be that strong. I suspect that to make \$400,000,000 it does have to be that strong, but I do not know. I have not earned that much money.

How to Develop Your Idea and Desire

If you do not already know, you will one day discover that the thoughts you put into your head have a huge influence on you and your life. Once you understand this, you realize that you can greatly influence your life by controlling the thoughts you allow inside in your head.

With this knowledge as a catalyst, here are the first steps you must take to obtain your desired amount of money. You will need to decide:

1. The Amount You Want

    The first step you must take is to decide how much money you want to have. You must answer the question, "How much money do I want to have? How much money do I desire?"

    Do not be flippant with your answer to this question. When I answered this question, I came up with an amount that seemed reasonable to me. I did not want to be too greedy, and I wanted to have an amount that seemed possible to obtain. Now, years after I asked myself this question, I have the exact amount of money I answered. My bank account has stayed at that amount of money for about five years now, wavering only slightly above or below the amount on occasion. It is as if an invisible force keeps me at that amount, and in fact, it does.

So, give this question some serious thought. What amount of money do you desire?

Once you have decided how much money you want, you must fixate on this amount of money. You must feel as if that money is coming to you, as if it is already yours. Money (energy) is out there. You must learn how to call it towards you and let it find its way to you. However, the first step is for you to let the World/Universe/Energy know how much you seek, how much you desire.

2.   What You Will Give

You must exchange something for the money. What are you going to give, create, and do in exchange for the Universe answering your call for your money? You must bring something of value to the world. What do you have that is of value? What can you create that will be of value? What are you going to do in exchange for your money?

3.   When You Need It

Is this something you can live without for ten years? Five years? Do you need it immediately? When do you need this money?

Some people like and need to have solid deadlines in order to accomplish anything. In my case, I did not really have a firm date in mind. I thought having my money within two or three years would be sufficient. However, because I was a bit "wishy-washy" on the time line, it took six years. Having a deadline can help spur you to action.

4. How You Will Get It

   Create a road map of the steps you will take to deliver what you decide to give in exchange for your money.

5. To Write it Down

   Commit all of the above onto a piece of paper. Write a clear, concise statement that says how much money you desire, what you will give in exchange for it, and by what date you will have it.

Desire Enough

By changing your desire level from "should" to "must," you summon energy to help you with your actions. You inform the Universe that something must and will happen.

By focusing your thoughts on your desired level of money, the idea(s) or actions you will exchange for this money, your level of urgency, and your time line and plans, you begin to develop the necessary foundation to start and complete the journey to your million dollars. Working on the pieces increases your desire to achieve your end goal—since developing the plan helps to make it real. Making it more real makes it more tangible, which increases your desire to make it happen.

In general, these are the first steps you will take to start you on your journey to your million dollars. For some reason, if your desire is strong enough, good things happen to you. For some reason, if your desire is strong enough, you find ways to make things happen. Why or how this occurs, we do not know. However, desire and determination, combined with faith, are powerful forces. When you combine them, you tell the Universe that something must happen.

Optional Action

The above information is sufficient to get you started with changing your mind-set and increasing your desire. If you would like additional information regarding mind-set and desire, visit HowToMakeaMillion.com for links to relevant material.

Think Big

To earn your million dollars, you have to think big. A million dollars is more than you have now, so you are headed towards a "bigger" financial situation. However, that is only one aspect of the thinking big that is required.

Throughout history the men who have made millions (or billions) of dollars affected more than one or two people. They affected hundreds, thousands, or millions of people. For you to earn your million you will also have to make a large impact.

There is no reason to limit yourself to small thinking. If you want a million dollars to come to you, you must think big. It is relatively easy to start a small business, but the money comes in large quantities only if you do something that affects many people. You must think big to earn big. You must do something that is major in some way, either in novelty or in the scope and size of the business.

A Small Candy Shop

One weekend when I was in the fifth grade, my friend and I rode our bicycles to the corner store and bought two boxes of grape tangy taffy candy. The next week we took the candy to school and kept it in our lockers. Between classes, we sold each piece of ten-cent taffy for the monopolistic price of $0.25. We made a 150 percent profit!

The following weekend we took our profits and returned to the candy shop. We repeated the process and again made a profit of 150 percent. From this, I learned the value of being a monopoly. There was no other source to buy candy in the school. What a great racket we had!

Thankfully, we did not get in trouble for our actions. The only real problem with the business was that instead of selling all the candy and reaping a cash reward, we tended to eat the last few bars ourselves after we had covered our costs.

This business was easy to run, but we did not make too much money from it. However, if we had decided to "think big" we could have made much more money. We only sold to kids in our class. Had we expanded our sales to kids in other classes we could easily have made five times our money. Had we expanded to other schools we would have multiplied our earnings even further. However, "thinking big" never occurred to us. We were just kids, after all.

Me vs. Steve Jobs

When I was a junior in high school, I wrote software for a few small businesses. Personal computers were new, and companies were just starting use them. The choices for software to use were very limited.

A video rental store opened near my house. Since I had a computer with which I could do the work, I asked them if they wanted me to print mailing labels for their customer list. They said yes, so I wrote a very simple mailing list program. Another company needed a simple word processing program, so I wrote one for them.

Realizing these programs had some value, I went door-to-door in a small office park with a flyer trying to get other companies to buy consulting services and programs from me. The problem with this approach was that I spent too much time on companies that had no (current) intention of buying a computer.

My approach is different from what Steve Jobs did when he started Apple Computer. When Jobs developed his first product, he went to an electronics store near his house. He asked the owner if he would be interested in purchasing a fully assembled computer circuit board. This board was, in essence, the core of a computer. The owner said he was definitely interested. In fact, he wanted fifty of them delivered as soon as possible. Jobs went back to his technology partner Steve Wozniak, and "Woz" assembled the boards. Apple Computer was born, and their first sale was fifty units.

What Jobs did was "think big." Unlike me, he "went to where the fish were." Jobs went to a spot where there were likely to be more customers for his idea. Everyone who entered the electronics store was likely to buy something. What I was doing at age eighteen was not thinking big. I was talking to one company at a time, sometimes educating them about what a computer could do for their business. Jobs talked to one storeowner and sold fifty units!

How to Think Big

The Internet allows you to communicate with almost anyone anywhere in the world for free. That is unprecedented in the history of the world. The effects on the business world have only just begun.

The impact of this on your ability to think big and take action to affect many people in a big way is an opportunity that is waiting for you to discover. The potential marketplace for your idea has expanded. It is now easy to communicate quickly and transact with people all over the world. Prior to the 1990s, this was not possible.

Think Like Billionaires: Consider Scope and Scale

If you want to be rich, it helps to think like rich people. In fact, it might be a requirement. So, what do some of the richest men in the world focus on when they think about business? They focus on scope and scale, and they definitely think big. They want the scope, or size, of the market to be very grand. Worldwide, if possible. They also want the business to be able to scale easily.

Scope

The scope of your opportunity is the size of your opportunity. In other words, just how big is your market? Just how big is what you are trying to do? Which portions of the market are you trying to serve and capture?

If you are selling grape taffy to kids at your school, the scope of your business is very small. If you are selling computer boards to every electronics store in the United States, the scope of your business is much larger. If you can follow up the sale of your computer board with an actual "personal" computer (the Apple 2e), then a groundbreaking computer (the Macintosh), then later the iPod, the iPad, and the iPhone, the scope of your business is gigantic.

For you to earn millions you need to think big. The scope and impact of your idea needs to be large. There is no reason to limit yourself to thinking small. There is an infinite amount of energy into which you can tap. You have the unprecedented opportunities of the Internet, should you need it.

Of course, it is possible to start small to perfect something (a business, product, or service) and then grow the business after it is ready. However, it must be possible to grow the business. Selling taffy to kids in your class is wonderful, but the scope is not enough to make a million dollars. Your million-dollar idea must have a scope larger than selling candy to a few local children.

Celebrities and sports stars earn huge money because of the scope of what they do. Millions of people watch and follow celebrities. For better or worse, they have a large impact. (Note: To achieve this they leverage stored wealth found in sports arenas and shiny movie theaters.)

If you make a small movie on your computer, you can show it to your friends and their families. You can also put it on YouTube for a slightly larger audience. However, to make a million dollars from a movie a very large audience must see it. You must have an idea and a plan that is "big" is some way to reach your million dollars.

So Think Big!

Scale

Scale refers to the ability of your small business to turn into a gigantic one. Will what you are doing at a small level work at a very, very large level?

A pizza company that makes everything by hand is more difficult to replicate and expand across the country and world than a McDonald's-type restaurant that has a very systematic and technological focus. It is easier to replicate the success of a McDonald's because they eliminate as much human error as possible from the process of making and delivering the food. They use the same machines, ingredients, and procedures in every restaurant.

If your million-dollar idea is something replicable like McDonald's, then you have a much better chance of growing your business to a grand scale than Bob's Homemade Pizza Shoppe. A babysitting or dog-walking referral service that works in one location will likely work easily in many others. The software used to run one business's location can be used in another location. However, the actual dog-walking service itself is more difficult to scale to other locations because you need people to walk the dogs.

What is the true size of the market for your idea? What is the size of the opportunity? Is it something you can accomplish with one product or service, or will you need to grow in size and product or service offerings over time?

If there is no market for your idea, you will not make much money from it. However, if there is a market, there is no reason to limit the size of your opportunity. With advent of the Internet, we are in an era where markets may exist anywhere in the world.

So Think Big!

Faith

I have always disliked the phrase "have faith." I never quite understood what it meant, and nobody explained it to me. It seemed to simply mean, "don't worry." Don't worry? I don't want "don't worry!" I want action, results, and success!

However, you must understand that you can and will achieve whatever it is that you decide to do as your million-dollar idea. Having "faith" means to trust the tried and true process, follow it "faithfully," and the Universe/God/Nature/Providence will provide what you seek. The process is the topic of this book.

Your subconscious picks up on signals sent from your conscious mind and your environment. If your conscious mind does not believe you will be successful, this thought passes to your subconscious mind—and then works on making that thought, that belief, true. However, if your subconscious mind picks up on clues that you are successful, then it will work to make that thought true. This will propel you towards success.

This is why what you put into your head is so important. Your thoughts, what you consciously choose to think about, influence your success and your future. So, if you want a million dollars, you need to direct your thoughts accordingly.

One aspect of the thinking required is that you must have faith in yourself and the process. If your journey to your million dollars is like mine, things will go wrong along the way. Things will waste your time. You must trust the process and have faith in it. You must believe and know that it will work, even if along the way you encounter temporary setbacks. The setbacks may slow you down, but the result will be good.

Faith in the Process Yields Millions

The day before Richard Branson started Virgin Airlines, he took their one airplane up for a test ride. A major problem occurred: one of the engines flamed out. Since the company did not officially start until the next day, the insurance was not active. The engine fire cost Branson $1,000,000. This is not a good way to start a company, but it did not deter Branson. He had faith. The airline went on to success despite losing one million dollars before it even started.

A man from Korea named Do Won Chang came to the greatest land of opportunity in the world (the United States of America) in 1981. To earn money he was a janitor, a gas station attendant, and worked in a coffee shop—all at the same time. It was difficult and low-paying work. However, after three years he had saved enough to open a clothing store. He had faith in the country and the process. Today his stores, Forever 21, are all over the world, with revenues over two billion dollars each year.

A man from Canada made money by walking on tall stilts and eating fire. He took a small troupe of performers all the way to Los Angeles for an arts festival. He had so much faith in his show and the process that he gambled everything he had—not even having enough money for a return ticket to Canada. That faith paid off for him, as this is how the world-famous Cirque du Soleil started. The man is now worth two billion dollars.

Confidence

For me this faith is more of a "feel" than anything else. I knew a GPS tour guide was a good idea that needed to be done by someone. I knew I was the perfect person to develop and deploy the system. I had complete confidence and faith in myself.

You must get into this same state of mind. You must know you are the perfect person for the job. You must know you can do it. You must know what you are exchanging for your million dollars has value, and you must be confident about it. If you are not confident, your subconscious mind will pick up on this—and you will radiate this lack of confidence. Other people will pick up on this signal and will not believe in you or your product or service.

You must go through the Universal process to get your idea, develop your team, develop your plans, etc. There are plenty of examples that show the process exists and how it works. These examples should help you develop the faith necessary to begin and continue your efforts.

If your mind-set is "this can never happen to me" or "this only happens to other people" (who are supposedly better, smarter, more talented, blah, blah, blah...), you must stop this destructive thinking immediately. You must have faith in the process and in yourself.

What you focus on, what you *think* about, is what you get. If you say "never me" then you are right. Good luck to you with that mind-set.

Avoiding "Bad Luck"

Have you ever met someone who seems to have an incredible amount of bad luck? Everything seems to be difficult for them. Business meetings that should yield sales suddenly fall apart. Family problems happen all the time. Payments from clients are difficult to obtain.

Examination of these people frequently shows that they have a negative mind-set. They think, "Things are always difficult—it takes a *lot* of work to succeed." This means the fact that they think things are difficult is in their subconscious. So, their subconscious, taking whatever was fed into it, works to make that thought a reality—and causes things to become more difficult.

This might seem far-fetched at first, but when you see so many negative things happen to the same person—you begin to wonder about the cause. A detrimental mind-set—thoughts that cause problems—is often the cause.

Your Choice

If you have ever had a daytime thought show up in your dreams at night, you understand that what you focus on during the day influences your thoughts at night. What you focus upon is what your brain works on, even while you sleep! So, if your mind-set is "never me" then your brain will work on "never me!" You will continue to fail—or at least not succeed as you wish. You certainly will not get a million dollars.

But if
- You focus on attracting money
- You focus on getting your million-dollar idea
- You focus on how to execute your plans
- You focus on how to sell your idea
- You focus on how to expand your efforts

... then these things are delivered to you. Your brain will tap into the infinite resources that exist (even while you are sleeping) and deliver to you a solution and a positive result.

You have to believe the process will work. You have to understand that the process will work, which it will! It is not "luck" at all. Have faith in the process and in yourself.

Developing Faith

The more you feel something, the more you know it is true. The more you experience something, the more you know it is true. The more it is true to you, the more you "believe" in it. The more you have faith in it.

A friend of mine did not believe in the mysterious "green flash" phenomena exhibited by the sun at sunset. Under certain circumstances, right as the last bit of the sun falls below the horizon, a flash of green light occurs. If you have not seen it, you might not believe it happens—but it does.

One evening looking out over the ocean at sunset, my friend finally saw the green flash. She suddenly believed in something that had always existed—because she had seen it happen herself. To believe in something it helps to experience it.

But how can you experience something if it does not happen to you? How can you "experience" your million dollars if you do not have it?

There is good news in the answer to these questions. You can feel like something happens to you without it actually happening to you!

Before you think this is crazy—ask anyone who has had a strong dream while sleeping about their experience. They can vouch for this: the experience felt real even though what was in their dream did not actually happen.

So, there are ways to "trick" yourself into feeling and believing things are real that are not yet real. It is possible to develop your belief and faith by taking advantage of this and other related facts.

The incantation section of this book is designed to help you develop your belief and your faith. Other material in this book is meant to do the same thing. Through your focused attention and actions, you will develop the needed faith and mind-set required to obtain your million dollars.

Have faith in yourself and have faith in the process.

What is in Your Head?

To increase your belief and faith, spend fifteen minutes every day focusing upon the fact that what you put in your head is what you, your brain, and your subconscious will focus upon and strive towards. During the fifteen minutes, ask yourself if you focused on anything detrimental recently. If so, just quickly acknowledge that it was a mistake to do so—and redirect your thoughts to positive thoughts. Focus on the amount of money you will acquire. Focus on obtaining your million-dollar idea. Focus on giving whatever it takes to achieve your goal.

Focus on having positive thoughts throughout your day. Think about all the positive and useful things that you will do when you have the money. Think about the people you will make happy via your new product, service, or idea.

These positive thoughts will develop and increase your self-confidence. You need people to assist you on your journey. If you are positive and confident, they will gladly assist you. If you believe in other people and have faith in them, they will be more likely to assist you.

You can also think about what it will be like to be successful and have your million dollars (or whatever amount you desire). How will you feel? What will you have? What will you do?

How solid will your confidence be? If you focus on these questions, you will "feel" like you have your million dollars. If you "feel" something, you experience it to some degree. If you experience something, it will increase your belief in it and help your faith in the process.

We do not know exactly how the process works, but believing or knowing you are going to do something greatly increases the chance of it happening. If you do not believe you can do something, then you cannot do it. You might not even try.

A Universal Truth

What you put into your head affects your development and future. What you think about influences many things, including your confidence. Your internal confidence reflects outwards, and other people see it and react to it. If your confidence is strong, this will benefit both you and them. People want to be around confident people. This means that your thoughts, which influence your confidence, also influence other people—and therefore your ability to execute your million-dollar plan.

In our Universe, these things—thoughts, future, confidence, belief, faith, results—are all related. This is a truth that cannot change. Your belief, faith, and thoughts all effect your confidence. Your current thoughts effect your future and your financial results. Your thoughts influence whether or not you will have a million dollars. Said more strongly, your thoughts can determine if you will have your million dollars. *It is up to you.*

You must have faith in yourself and in the Universal process described in this book. With this combined faith, you are prepared to utilize a Universal truth and tap into energy that is available to you. When you do, the path you are on is the same taken by countless others who have made millions of dollars.

A Backpacker Finds Shoes

A young man went on a vacation in Argentina. He was living in California and wondering what to do next in his life. On his vacation, he encountered some simple "Alpargata" shoes. He took several pairs back to Los Angeles and asked his fashion friends how much they would pay for the shoes. They said up to $50. Blake Mycoskie knew he could purchase the shoes in Argentina for less than $5. TOMS Shoes was born and went on to sell millions of pairs of shoes—and donate millions of pairs of shoes to needy children and adults, all over the world.

Notice Mycoskie was asking the Universe what to do next in his life. His thoughts were focused specifically on his future. The Universe responded with an answer to his question. He did some initial research with his friends and then decided to start a business. He developed a plan and followed his plan to great success.

A Man with Faith in a "Gold Mine" Idea

A man named John Johnson grew up in the 1920s in a poor section of Arkansas. In 1933, his family moved to Chicago to give him more opportunity. In high school, he worked on the school newspaper and the class yearbook.

He finished school and had an idea for a publication patterned after the then popular "Reader's Digest." He planned to call his magazine "Negro Digest." He felt that this idea was a "black gold mine." Many people discouraged him from pursuing his idea but he ignored them and kept working on his plan. He had desire, he had an idea, and he had faith in himself and his plan.

His mother also believed in her son. She had so much faith in him that she allowed him to use their furniture as collateral for a $500 loan for the magazine. In 1942, he produced his first publication, and it was successful.

Wanting more, Johnson decided to start another new magazine. He called it "Ebony." It focused on successful black Americans and the first issue sold out immediately. He had found his true gold mine. The magazine was extremely successful and influential—and eventually reached a circulation level of 2.3 million readers.

If he and his mother did not have the required faith in themselves, Johnson may have listened to his detractors. If he did not have faith in his "gold mine" of an idea, he may have given up on his plans. Instead, his desire to succeed drove him onward—and Johnson became one of the richest men in the United States.

To encourage you to have faith in yourself, Johnson wrote a message to you in his autobiography. It says, "If it could happen to a Black Boy from Arkansas it could happen to anyone."

The Process

Faith, desire, an idea, and a plan are all elements of the process Johnson used to become very successful. The story of TOMS Shoes has similar elements. There are countless examples of men making millions using this process.

There is no reason you should not be one of these men. There is nothing that can stop you from deciding what you want, developing a strong desire, and having faith in the process. It will work for you. This is how it is done. It is a truth from the Universe.

Your Thoughts About Money

Presumably, you have decided that you want one million dollars to come to you. Have you thought about what this really means? Where does it come from? Why does it come to some people but not to others? There are many questions related to money other than the obvious "How do I get some?"

The answers to the questions are as simple or complex as you wish them to be. But to acquire your million dollars it helps to understand this: *money is energy.*

In order to understand how much energy is out there, think about all the things that are possible because of energy. Each plant on the face of the earth thrives because of the energy from the sun. There are not an infinite number of plants on earth, but there are a very large number. Other plants preceded those plants and yet more plants will replace them. All of them tap into the sun's energy to live. An infinite amount of energy sustains the plants.

If you watch waves crash on a shoreline, only to retreat again, only to crash again, only to retreat again, only to crash again, you might marvel at the beauty, but you can also see an ongoing energy source. The country of Norway generates most of its electricity using water. Meanwhile solar panels tap into the sun's energy, which potentially provides the rest of the world with an infinite supply of electricity.

These are basic examples of humans tapping into energy sources. The point is relative to humans: there is certainly an infinite amount of energy available into which we can tap. It is helpful to understand the "Money is Energy" truism when you are attracting money to you. You are not attracting pieces of paper (green paper in the United States); you are attracting energy to you—and there is an infinite amount of energy out there from which you can attract as much as you desire.

Why is Money Energy?

You might be asking yourself, "why is money energy and what does this have to do with me getting a million dollars?" To answer that question, let us first talk about financial wealth. How does a person become financially "wealthy?"

Imagine two cavemen sitting in front of their campfire. They have the capability and energy to hunt, fish, eat, sleep, etc. They have minimal wealth, maybe just a few tools and an animal skin or two to keep them warm. They also have their God/Nature/Providence given energy to get them up in the morning and get them through the day.

If they continue their daily routines, their wealth does not increase much. Maybe they gain a few fish from a successful spearing session.

Then one day, one of the cavemen somehow gets the idea to build some small lean-to shacks made out of trees. He builds an extra one for his fellow caveman—and this caveman gives the builder some fish from his day's catch in exchange for the new warmer, drier home.

The two men just became wealthier. How did they do this? They could have sat around doing nothing for the entire day. This would not have increased their wealth. Instead, they both used their energy to produce something of value. Then they exchanged their products, benefiting both of them.

So, building wealth is using your energy to create something of value. You exchange your *energy* for something of *value*.

Some people use their energy to produce houses. Some produce fish. Others produce other things. In order to facilitate the exchange of goods, we invented money. It is difficult to carry around a wallet full of fish. It is easier for everyone to agree to exchange money when we exchange things of value. It makes the transactions much easier. So instead of exchanging things of value directly, we exchange money for things of value. The recipient of the money can then exchange it for something else of value.

But we have already discovered that something of value used to be energy. Somebody changed their energy into something of value. So, exchanging things of value for money is exchanging energy for money. Money represents energy. Money is energy.

This might seem a little strange or far-fetched when you first think about it. But it is very helpful to understand when you are seeking to acquire your million dollars. You are actually trying to acquire energy. And as already seen in this chapter, there is an infinite amount of energy available in our world. Why should you not have a small (million-dollar) piece of that infinite energy? The amazing thing is that if you ask for it in the correct manner, the money, the energy will come to you.

Back to humans building wealth: as time goes on, as long as conditions are favorable (e.g., no famine, plagues, mass diseases, major wars) human wealth increases and accumulates. For example, men exchange energy to build roads. The roads last for some time, benefiting many people by allowing them to travel and work on projects in other areas of the land and build homes and office buildings. The first wealth produced, the roads, are still there. On top of that accumulated wealth (energy) we later build more wealth as evidenced by new homes and buildings.

Do not forget, the original source of all financial wealth is man's God-given energy that men agree to change into something of value. In this manner, we transform energy into things of value. Through this process, energy is accumulated and stored.

Alexander Graham Bell changed his energy into a telephone. Someone else invented a computer. For a while, everyone used telephone lines to transmit information between computers, combining two useful and valuable inventions. Now, computer information "flies through the air" via satellite transmissions.

These advances allow us access to more information than ever before in the history of the world. The information is valuable, which means the wealth of humans is increasing.

Energy/Money/Wealth

We have seen there is an infinite amount of energy around us and available to us. We see that humans are accumulating wealth (energy). Because of this, there is more and more energy/wealth available to us as time goes on because people are changing some of their energy into things of value, which "store" the energy.

All of this should help you realize that acquiring a million dollars (energy) is quite possible and actually not that big of a deal. What you are seeking is abundantly available.

In order to acquire your million dollars, you simply have to develop and execute a plan to acquire your million dollars. This sounds ridiculously simple, but I assure you in some ways it is not. There is more to it than that. Many people want to have a million dollars. If it were simple to acquire the money, more people would have it.

However, it is clear the money/energy is out there waiting to be acquired. There is an infinite amount of resources available for you to use. There is an infinite amount of energy/money available from which you can extract whatever amount you wish.

How to extract your million dollars is discussed throughout this book, including in this chapter.

Energy is Responsibility

Once you have your pile of money, be it a million dollars or more, you will realize that it does represent energy. When you have this money, you have the energy resources available to you to do many things. You can use your money/energy to build a building. You can finance a movie. You can go to a tropical island and drink margaritas.

When you have a million dollars, you realize you have accumulated energy and therefore have the power to make things happen that you could not before you had the money. Money/energy has come to you and you are now the keeper and custodian of that energy.

You can use the energy for whatever purpose you want. It is an important responsibility. But when you are seeking to acquire your money it helps to understand it is energy—and you are asking the Universe, which is full of energy, to give some to you. You are asking to be the keeper and custodian of some of the energy from the Universe.

This is not meant, by any means, to sound like "new age" jargon. Remember, your author is writing from experience and has a scientific background. This "money is energy" mantra is something that cannot be explained or understood fully. However, my experience and that of many other millionaires shows there is something positive and beneficial to this thinking.

Keep an open mind. There are things you do not fully understand. There are things nobody fully understands. But the mind-set and methodology discussed in this book work for those that desire to pursue their millions.

Your Attitude Towards Money

"Money is the root of all evil," so the saying goes. Regardless of whether this is true, it does not mean money is evil.

In order to attract your million dollars, you must have a positive attitude about money. It is possible you have an attitude about money and wealth that is not conducive to your receiving your million dollars. In order for you to receive your million dollars, this must change.

Having money is not a bad thing. However, we hear negative comments about "rich people" (often from vote-hungry politicians), and people sneered at them. If you do not have money, this gives you a good excuse for not having it. Your thinking may be this: if you had a million dollars, you would be one of those "evil rich people," and of course, you are not one of them. Therefore, you are happy you are not like them.

This is both a convenient excuse for having not earned a million dollars—and something that prevents you from actually receiving a million dollars. Because you are happy you are not one of them, you will not become one of them. You will not be rich.

You must want to have a million dollars before you earn your million dollars. The process of acquiring your million dollars starts with that desire.

What Do You Really Think About Money?

Your thoughts influence money coming to you, and your experiences influence your thoughts. Because of this, some people need to examine their family's money history to see if any experiences are influencing their current thoughts about money.

Some people have deep-rooted thoughts in their heads about money—thoughts that will prevent them from acquiring much of it. Something in their experience causes them to associate negativity with money, which prevents them from wanting to have it.

Examine your experiences with money and see if you have any negative thoughts associated with being rich. Were your parents often arguing about money? Did these arguments cause stress? If you see money as a source of stress, then you may subconsciously want to avoid having much of it. If you associate money with fighting, then you likely have a thought in your head that money equals fighting. Obviously, that type of thought is detrimental to having money come to you.

Did someone you know have a lot of money and your parents, teachers, or other people who influenced you resented that person? Did you grow up in a wealthy area and have other people make assumptions about you because of it? If wealth has been a source of derision or resentment in your life, you might subconsciously be avoiding these things by avoiding wealth. Again, that type of thought is not conducive to money coming to you.

Can you make more money than your father makes? Some men with strong fathers have a mental block against making more money than their fathers make. On the other hand, some men have a mental spark that drives them to make more money than their fathers.

From these examples, you begin to see how your thoughts could influence what you think about money and how they might influence your having money. Examine your thoughts to make sure yours are positive in regard to making a million dollars. If you have any negative thoughts about money, you will need to correct them before your million dollars can come to you.

Good People with Money

Money does not make you evil. One of the richest men I ever met pays the college tuition for one hundred students every year. Another extremely wealthy man I know donates large sums of money each year to several health research companies who work to cure diseases. One of the richest men in the U.S., who has repeatedly made hundreds of millions with technology companies, gives his personal technological help to startup companies so they can succeed as he did.

All of these men are great examples that money does not make you evil. In fact, the opposite can be true. If the men did not have their millions, none of their good deeds would exist; the kids would not get their college tuition paid, the researchers would not find cures for diseases, the companies would not get a chance to prove their worth. So, the millions of dollars are far from "evil!" The money is extremely helpful and beneficial!

Today, many, if not most, college students are subjected to anti-rich propaganda. Yet their colleges and universities, as well as other charities, regularly receive donations from "evil rich people." These donations do not receive much press coverage. However, the donations are made because at some place and time someone spent their energy in pursuit of money, in pursuit of becoming rich. Once wealthy, the benefactors do good things with their money and donate to their favorite causes.

The school's alumni focused their thoughts on being successful. They received their money from the Universe and now can donate to their school or charity of choice. That is what rich people can do.

What to Think About Money

You must be happy and comfortable with your pursuit of your million dollars. You must be comfortable with having a million dollars. You must not be ashamed of your desire for your money.

The money will allow you to have the life you dream of— and allow you to donate to the charity or cause of your choice, if you wish. Or you may use your money to do something else of benefit to people. Your money is a good thing!

Think of all the good things your money will allow you to do (beyond paying your rent!). The things you think of are in your future. That goodwill come from you wanting and then receiving your million dollars. Money is evil? Not at all!

Let it Come to You

To receive your million dollars, you must begin to welcome money coming to you. Money is energy and the world is full of energy. You want to attract this money to you, so do not do anything to dissuade it from coming to you.

If you are doing a business deal, raise your price without hesitation. The money should come to you and wants to come to you. So why should you leave any money on the table? In fear of being called greedy? Why should you not want a larger chunk of energy (money) from the world that has an abundant amount of energy? Ask for more. You can lower the price later if needed, but your time on the earth is short—so ask for your price now.

Expect, imagine, and think about receiving money from any source. You might find $100 lying on the sidewalk. A stock you purchased might increase in value. A client might call with a "rush job" for which they will pay double your normal rate. These occurrences are positive events that benefit you. They are the types of things that can happen when you are comfortable with money—and are in the mind-set of attracting money to you.

These "small" occurrences of money coming to you will happen once you start to think positively about money. Then your million-dollar idea is going to come to you and bring you however much money you desire, too. But first you have to be ready to receive money—and your idea(s) that become money. How you will receive your idea is covered later in this book. For now, we focus on your attitude about money.

When you expect something—it can happen. So, cultivate a positive attitude towards money. Imagine it coming to you. Welcome it coming to you. It is your friend. Imagine opening up your bank account and seeing the full amount of money you desire in your account.

Action

To aid you in becoming used to having lots of money—spend some time in fancy shops that sell items for large amounts of money. Imagine yourself purchasing the items, because you will soon be able to do so. If there are no fancy shops near you, get a copy of the *Robb Report* magazine.

Meanwhile, if possible, spend time around rich people. Many good things may happen from this:

- You will develop some of their same habits
- You may develop a network of contacts which might be help you earn your million dollars
- You will become more comfortable with money and being around money
- You will increase your subconscious' expectation that you will have money
- You will realize that "rich" people have many of the same characteristics that you do

You will realize that *you* know some things that they do not! (Knowing something other people do not can be very lucrative.)

When you "daydream" about buying expensive items and doing the same things rich people do—it has an influence on your subconscious mind. Your subconscious feels these activities as if they are real—and begins to think you already have the money. This helps you become more comfortable with it. This in turn helps to attract money to you.

Spend some time thinking about and "feeling" money. Imagine you have your million dollars in your bank account. See the dollar figures on your bank statement balance. What would you do with your money? Where would you go on a daily basis? Imagine how you would feel with the money in your possession.

Many possible emotions can come with having the money. What emotions resonate with you? How do you feel with a million dollars in your bank account?

If you are not comfortable with money, it will not come to you. The power that hands out money senses (or knows) that you are not comfortable with it. You are not ready for it. So, the money/energy does not come to you. When you pretend you have the money and "feel" it, you begin to get comfortable with it.

Always Accept It

To demonstrate to the Universe that you are comfortable with money—and ready for it—you should always accept it. Let it come to you.

If you find yourself in a situation where somebody offers you more money than you think they should, accept the money with a "thank you!" There is no virtue in refusing to accept money/energy from the Universe—in fact the opposite may be true. Refusing the money insinuates that something is "bad" or wrong about the money. This is not true! Money is energy and allows you to do good things. Do not refuse it, accept it!

If someone offers you a monetary tip for some reason, accept the money with a "thank you!" Even if the amount is small, the positive monetary transaction helps put you in the right frame of mind to obtain your million dollars.

Why is this important? Famous American author Ralph Waldo Emerson captured the reason in this quote:

> *The ancestor of every action is thought; when we understand that we begin to comprehend that our world is governed by thought and that everything without had its counterpart originally within the mind.*

He is saying thought influences every one of man's actions. Every one of man's creations was first a thought. So, every man-made object or service is influenced by thought. If your thoughts about money are not comfortable, this influences your actions in regard to money. This, in turn, has a great impact on whether or not money comes to you.

Comfort plus Desire

Gaining comfort around money is one of the required steps you must take on your path to your million dollars. Combining comfort around money with a strong desire to have a million dollars creates a base from which you will be propelled towards your million dollars.

After you establish this base, you need a million-dollar idea.

How to Get Your Million-Dollar Idea

One night when I was in college, my roommate and I stayed up doing homework. I worked on math problems while he worked on physics problems. We worked very hard and concentrated on the homework for several hours. At 11 p.m., we went to bed.

At 2 a.m., I woke up because he jumped out of his bed and turned on his lamp. He sat at his desk and scribbled down the answer to a particularly difficult physics problem that he worked on before going to bed. Then he turned off the light and went back to sleep.

Have you ever woke up at 2 a.m. with the answer to a physics problem in your head? Probably not. So why did this happen to him?

The answer to this question is important to you on your journey to your million dollars. You must understand the answer, or at least utilize its implications, to acquire your money.

Your Subconscious

The obvious answer to the "Why did this happen to him?" question is, of course, because he was working on physics problems, and he came up with one of the answers. That is how you solve homework problems. However, the problem with this answer is that he was not working on the problem when he came up with the answer. He was asleep in his bed!

So, why did the answer come to him? Why, instead of dreaming about being on the beach of a tropical island or dreaming about meeting Marilyn Monroe or something along those lines, did my roommate receive the answer to a physics problem and then woke up to write it down? The answer is my roommate had accidentally tapped into an amazing source of wealth, creativity, and ideas—his subconscious mind.

Nobody knows exactly how the subconscious mind works. But yours is an incredible source of dreams, ideas, thoughts, and catalysts to action—working exclusively for and available only to you. You will use it to get your million dollars.

What is Hypnosis?

To understand better what happened with my roommate— and the process through which you can acquire your million dollars—it helps to examine a few things that may have happened in your life and the phenomena that some people call "hypnosis."

Some people describe hypnosis as simply staying in the state or condition you pass through every night when you go to sleep and every morning when you wake up. The state occurs when you are half awake and half asleep. Given that definition, everyone is "hypnotized," even if just for a few moments, each night and morning. This means hypnotizing someone is the process of putting someone into that state and keeping them there, rather than having them fall into a deeper sleep.

Perhaps while sleeping and dreaming you have had an external stimulus (e.g., noise from an alarm clock, a person touching you lightly) incorporated into your dream. That is, something from the "real world" was incorporated into the thoughts you had during your dream. You experienced something "real" (the noise) and something "unreal" (the dream) at the same time. This melding of "real world" and "dream world" is, or is at least an element of, hypnosis.

If you have experienced such a dream, you may then realize your conscious mind (which hears the noise) can influence your subconscious mind. Your subconscious mind is always at work. It controls your dreams and other thinking, even when you are asleep. It creates new ideas and thoughts and it can work with stimuli passed to it by your conscious mind. (That is why the beep from your alarm clock can be incorporated into your dream.) In this way (and others), your conscious mind works with and influences your subconscious mind.

It is very important to understand this: *Your conscious mind influences your subconscious mind.*

It does not matter if you believe in hypnosis or not. You do not need to believe in it to make your million dollars. However, it is extremely helpful to understand that *real-world stimuli can and does influence dreaming and subconscious thinking.*

This knowledge is important because you can control your conscious mind. You control your thoughts, or at least, you can if you want to do so. *Because you can control your conscious thoughts, you can use your conscious mind to influence what your subconscious mind focuses upon.*

This is Your Key

This is what happened with my roommate and his physics homework. The external reality of his focus on his physics homework influenced his subconscious mind. Then while he slept, his subconscious mind went to work on that which had received so much focused thought when he and his conscious mind were awake.

Hours after he fell asleep, his subconscious mind found the answer to the physics problem. It was so important to him (i.e., it had received so much focused thought and concentration in his conscious mind) that his subconscious brain convinced him to wake up (become conscious again) and write down the answer.

Your subconscious mind can solve technical problems such as physics problems. Your subconscious mind can also create highly imaginative thoughts—as exemplified by the amazing things you see and experience in your dreams. Some people dream about flying. Some dream about paralysis. Others dream about being chased. You know which things you have dreamed about—when your subconscious imagination was at work.

When you are truly ready to begin your journey to your million dollars, you will use your conscious thought to influence your subconscious thinking. You will use the amazing facility that is your subconscious mind—which can give you, while in a dream, the experience of flying—to *give you your million-dollar idea.*

Given the right tools, your subconscious mind can solve many problems. In the case of my roommate, the tools were his preexisting knowledge of physics combined with a specific problem to work on. He focused on the physics problem, and then his subconscious mind took off and solved the problem given the tools with which it had to work.

In your case, your tools are your preexisting life knowledge, including any specialized knowledge you have. This knowledge combines with conscious focus on the homework problem, which activates your subconscious and focuses *it* on your homework problem. Your subconscious mind then, when it is ready, gives you the answer to your problem. However, your homework is not a physics problem. Your problem is "What will I do in exchange for my million dollars?"

How to: Your Incantation

So, when you are ready, start a daily ritual. An "incantation," if you wish to call it that, which will summon or direct your subconscious mind to provide you with the solution to your homework problem of "What will I do in exchange for my million dollars?" You have already started this, at least in part, if you took action after reading the chapter on "Desire." You are reminded here that you can act or not upon this advice as you wish. It is up to you. But it requires desire, faith, and *action* (and more) to obtain a million dollars.

You will use your conscious thoughts to focus on this problem. You will do this each night prior to going to bed and every morning when you wake up. You can also do this occasionally throughout the day any time you wish or have the opportunity to do so.

The more time and energy you consciously spend on the problem, the more time and energy your subconscious will spend on it. That is why additional time spent on the problem (not just morning and evening) is helpful. The more you focus on the problem, the more intensity you give to your thinking, the more energy your subconscious mind will direct towards the problem.

When you focus on the problem, you are telling your subconscious it is important and requires an answer. So, conduct your thinking and focus sessions with purpose and conviction, as if it is something that is important to you and your life—because it is.

When you do this each evening and each morning, it influences your subconscious to focus on the problem. It says to your subconscious, "No, really, this *is important*, and I must have a solution." This keeps your subconscious spending at least some of its time on the problem.

To aid you in this process, it might help to write down the exact thoughts and sentences you wish to pass through your conscious mind to your subconscious. The exact words and thoughts you should use need to come from you—which is why this text does not provide a specific set of sentences for the purpose, although an idea or two is suggested shortly.

Any Specific Requirements?

As part of this process, you need to include any required parameters you have in your specific situation. For example, maybe you can only work on your pursuit of your million dollars at night. In this case, you must have in your thoughts that the business or project must be viable at night.

Other examples could be a requirement that the solution works in a certain country or industry in which you need to operate. You can also specify that your solution incorporate some specialized knowledge that you have or want to acquire and use. Your specifics will come from your life, so put some thought into this before you arrive at the final words, sentences, and thoughts you use.

Some people might include a time line or end date delineating the time by which you need the money. Is it a short-term idea you need? Something that will take a year? Ten years? The rest of your working life? Some people are not looking only for a million dollars, but also something worthwhile that they can do until they retire.

Once you have thought through what should be included in your "incantation," write it down. The act of writing down your thoughts or sentences regarding what you need is helpful in passing this information to your subconscious mind. It also helps with reinforcement as you can read the exact same sentences morning and night and deliver them to your subconscious mind repetitively for processing. Keep the paper close to your bed and use it as a reminder to conduct your ritual.

Then each evening and each morning, read and concentrate on your situation and your "problem" as contained in what you wrote. "Talk" to your subconscious. Then, think a bit more and "feel" yourself working on whatever solution is delivered to you (even though you do not yet have the solution).

Imagine what your new life will be like. Feel what it will be like to be working on your million-dollar idea and delivering the results. Remember that you are comfortable with the money that is yours; it is just not yet with you. It is part of your life. It is part of you.

Do this faithfully. Keep it up daily. Have faith and wait.

There are things in life we do not understand. Nobody knows exactly how this process works, but the result may astonish you.

Tried and True

Does anyone really know how gravity works? You drop an object and it falls down. We know this is true. We know how fast an object will fall and know it speeds up as it falls, but we really do not know why. However, that does not mean gravity does not work.

Likewise, we do not know exactly how this process influences your subconscious mind—or how your subconscious mind solves problems. We just know it does.

Here are some facts: You certainly have a creative subconscious. You know this if you have ever had a dream while sleeping. You certainly have conscious thoughts that can be used to influence your subconscious thoughts. You have experience and knowledge that nobody else in the world has, which allows you to think of ideas that others will not. All of these things combined with the process outlined above can give you whatever you ask for.

Countless people throughout history have used this process. It is tried and true, yet it is not taught in our schools or universities. The process is laid out above. Follow it, and you will be another step closer to your million dollars.

My Story

To get my million-dollar idea, I started as discussed above. I knew I was ready for the idea. I needed the idea. I was ready to work on it. I knew roughly how much money I wanted. I knew I wanted to work on the idea right away—and I was living in New York City, so I needed to be able to work on it there.

I spent about two or three weeks in my apartment focusing my brain on the problem. I needed an idea for a business or a project that would make me my money. Every night, I would focus on the fact that I needed a major business or project on which to work to make my money. I repeated to myself that I was ready for it and needed it. I was ready for the millions of dollars. I was ready to do the work. I simply needed a good idea, and I would work on it and make it happen once I received it.

I thought all of these things and sometimes said them aloud: "I am ready and able to receive the money. I am ready to work on the idea that is delivered to me. I am excited to work on the project and to have the money. I am excited, ready, and willing to move into my new life." I repeated some version of these things to myself nightly and on most mornings.

For two weeks, I perceived no positive changes. I thought a bit more during some days about what my idea should be, but nothing concrete materialized. I did not think about the fact that nothing happened. It did not worry me at all. I had faith in the process—and of course, knew I did not have anything to lose by doing what I was doing. So, I continued.

Then came a day I will never forget.

It was a cold, sunny December afternoon in New York City. I had finished my Christmas shopping and had a free afternoon to do whatever I wanted to do. Christmas time in NYC is wondrous and enjoyable. It is pleasant to see people out and about, so I decided to go to the Metropolitan Museum of Art up on Fifth Avenue.

The purpose of going there was twofold. First, to see visitors from all over the world. Second, to find inspiration from the art. Some of the art is ancient, some more recent, but all of it was produced by men who worked and focused intensely to create something that years later people still line up to see.

The people and things you surround yourself with have an impact on you. Your thoughts influence your life. I thought thinking about and seeing creative art would help me to create something. I was looking to be inspired.

At the museum ticket desk, I rented an audio-guide device that explained some of the more popular art pieces. You carry the device with you—and find a piece of art with a number on the wall next to it. You type the number into the device and listen through the headset to learn about the piece of art.

As I walked up the large marble staircase inside the museum, I unrolled the wire from the headset. "This is a cool device," I thought, "Somebody should do this for all of New York City." Then, just as I reached the top of the steps, a bolt of lightning hit me: "That somebody is me."

The audio device would not work outside in New York City, as I was sure nobody would let you affix numbers to different points-of-interest throughout the city. Instead, it would have to use GPS (Global Positioning Satellites) to know where you were. "That might work," I thought. "Wait," I thought, "it would work!"

At that moment, at the top of the steps in the Met Museum, I knew I was the perfect person to work on the system. I knew I had my idea. My efforts to come up with a good idea worked perfectly.

In Your Case

The specifics of your idea will be different from mine. However, the process you go through will be similar. You need to focus on getting your idea. You need to tell your subconscious mind any details it needs to know about your situation and the idea that you need.

Maybe you need an idea that works well in the winter, for example. Or maybe it needs to be a summertime operation. Or maybe it has to be in a certain field such as farming or computers or travel or retail marketing or... whatever it is that you need. It is good to focus on an area you enjoy and/or in which you have specialized knowledge. (In my case I did not give a field to my subconscious mind—it simply scanned through my experience and said to me, "Hey, a GPS tour guide is a good idea.")

After you focus on the problem for a sufficient amount of time, your subconscious will deliver the answer to you. You will know it when you receive it. It might come to you in a dream. It might come to you while you are walking up a flight of stairs or while driving your car. You do not know when, where, or how the idea will come to you, but how it comes to you does not matter.

Nobody understands how this process works. You focus energy towards a thought (a problem) and your subconscious reaches out to somewhere to obtain the answer. It receives (or creates) the answer and delivers it to your conscious thought. No mortal man has an explanation for this amazing, wondrous process. But it works.

When your idea arrives, welcome it. You have been blessed with your answer and your new friend, this wonderful idea. Treat it with the joy it deserves. It will be with you for quite some time, and you will remember it for the rest of your life. So, welcome it.

Then get to work.

What Next?

It does not matter when, where, or how you receive your idea. But it matters greatly what you do next. You *must* take immediate action to move your idea forward. Hopefully your level of desire and excitement is so high that this will not be difficult.

In my case, I could barely wait to get back to my apartment to begin the work. It excited me. I needed to know if someone had already created a GPS tour guide. This could have shot down my business before it started. I started my research that evening. I searched online looking for news articles, businesses, advertisements—anything that would tell me if someone had already developed my idea.

But before I did that, I wandered around the Met Museum and looked at art.

Initial Research

Immediately after you are blessed with your (potential) million-dollar idea, it is time for you to conduct some initial research. You need to answer several questions in order to help you decide if your idea is viable, worthwhile, and something with which you can make your million dollars. These questions include:

Has someone already done this?

Has anyone done something similar?

Did they fail? If so, why?

Can you do it better (cheaper, faster, higher quality, more appealing, etc.) than they did?

Why can you do it better than them?

What skills or resources do you have that they did not?

Or:

Were they successful? How and why?

Did they acquire a patent for some essential piece of their business?

Are you prohibited from copying what they did?

Will what they did work for you?

How can you do it better than they did?

How can you do it differently than they did?

If nobody has ever done what you are proposing, why has nobody done it before?

Is it possible?

Is there a market for your proposed product or service?

How big is the market? How many people might want your product or service?

What will they be willing to pay for your product or service?

How much will it cost to provide your product or service?

Can you make money with those numbers?

Are there any technological impediments to your product or service?

Are there any governmental or social impediments that might prevent your idea from working?

The point of all these questions is to help you figure out if you should continue working with this specific brilliant idea. You are about to start down a path that will require intense focus, require your precious energy, and change your life forever. You are about to pass the point of no return with this idea. So, it makes sense to do a little research and make sure it really is a great idea and that you can work with it before investing your precious time, energy, and money.

Research Tool

One place to check to see if someone is already executing your idea is on the gust.com website. At: gust.com/search you can enter keywords to search for—and (if you choose to search for companies) you receive a list of companies that match on your search terms. You may find a company doing exactly what you are thinking about and/or you may find variations of your idea.

It might be a good thing to find that someone is already executing your idea or something similar. If someone is already making money doing what you are thinking about, then it proves there is a market for the idea. (Remember, just because somebody is in business does *not* mean they are making money)

If someone operates a business in your area that makes money, you can learn from what they have done. You can examine their marketing approach and/or copy other aspects of their business that work.

On the other hand, if someone has already acquired a patent on your idea or is established to such a degree that you cannot compete with them, it will require a different approach on your part to be successful. You can adjust your plan accordingly.

Reusing a Good Idea

If someone has already done something similar to your idea, study their results carefully. It might be possible that you can replicate their success by doing something similar or avoid their failure by doing something differently.

Mark Cuban made millions of dollars by "packaging" live sports radio streams on the Internet. It worked so well that after he "cashed out" on the project he decided to do the exact same thing again, except using the newer technology of video streams. Repeating something that someone already did successfully but in a different market, area, or manner might be a good idea. It may be a safer, more sound, and less stressful way to earn your million dollars compared to doing something completely new. Of course, it depends on what you have as your million-dollar idea.

My Story—Idea Confirmation

After I received my bolt-of-lighting idea while standing in the Metropolitan Museum in New York City, I raced home to do some research.

My first question was "Has anyone already done this?" I searched the Internet and found only one working GPS tour guide product. In San Francisco, on the northern end of Silicon Valley, someone had created a GPS tour guide company called "Go Car Tours." Their business involved renting small cars equipped with GPS tour guide systems to tourists. At the time, the business was new, and it did not appear that anyone else anywhere had a similar system.

It was clear to me their system was not appropriate for New York City. Driving the little vehicles in Manhattan was a death wish. Meanwhile, the way the vehicle-based system delivered information to the tourists would not work for people walking the streets of NYC. Therefore, their system was not useful for my situation.

Since they were the only established GPS tour guide business in the world, I decided my pedestrian GPS tour guide business would be the first of its type in the world. So far so good.

Next, I needed to know if a pedestrian GPS tour guide system would work in NYC. Tall buildings interfere with GPS signals, so I had to know how accurate the signals were down in the caverns of the "concrete jungle" of the city. If someone stands in Times Square, do the GPS signals say they are in Central Park? An error like that would make the system unworkable.

Before I could answer this question, I had to obtain a handheld device that read GPS signals. At the time, cell phones existed, but they did not have GPS capability. I researched devices and bought a handheld "PDA" computer that had a slot into which you could insert an external GPS antenna/reader device.

With the device in hand, I quickly set out to become the world's leading expert on GPS signals in New York City. I took the subway up to Times Square. I knew the device had to work there since all tourists in NYC visit Times Square.

I exited the underground station and walked to the corner of 42nd Street and Broadway. It was January and very cold. I was not excited to take off my winter gloves, but the touch screen would not work if I was wearing my gloves. I removed my gloves and turned on the device.

My hands turned cold and red as the device acquired GPS satellite signals. I did not know it then, but I was waiting to acquire signals from four satellites, the minimum required to calculate a location.

After about a minute, the device calculated a latitude and a longitude for my position and produced a reading. The map software showed I was standing in front of the Hard Rock Cafe. The restaurant was close to my position, but not precisely where I was actually standing.

I spent the next hour running around a freezing Times Square. My initial results repeated wherever I conducted a test. The GPS coordinates were fairly close to my actual location, but not always exactly where I was located.

In the next few days, I tested the device in all the touristy locations of Manhattan. The results were the same everywhere, except for the Wall Street area. In "older" parts of NYC, the buildings are closer together, and the streets are narrower. This creates concrete "tunnels" which affect the accuracy of GPS signals more than in other parts of the city. The area around Wall Street has this problem.

After my research, I knew more than anyone else did in the world about the accuracy of GPS signals in New York City. The signals delivered location readings that were "in the vicinity of" the actual location, but not perfect. My system, were I to develop it, would have to solve that problem.

The Solution

It took me a day or two of thinking to arrive at the "obvious" answer to the problem. By listing on the screen of the device all of the points-of-interest that were "nearby" to your location, you would inevitably list the point-of-interest which you were standing in front of. The maximum error of the GPS signals seemed to be around 1,000 feet—so if the system listed any point-of-interest within 1,000 feet of the user's calculated location, then the point-of-interest in which they were interested (standing in front of) would be listed on the screen.

In practice, this works easier than described in a book. What is important is that with the "Nearby" screen in my head, I had a workable concept for my GPS tour guide system. The system would work. It was feasible. It was a good idea. The technology would permit it to work. My initial research paid off with a good result:

I was going to create the world's first handheld GPS tour guide.

Your Research

Your story of earning your million dollars will be different from mine, but you will follow the same general steps. You will come up with your million-dollar idea and then you will research it to see if it has already been done and/or if it is feasible for you to do your version of it.

It is very possible that during your initial research you will learn things that improve your idea. Knowledge is a very useful tool—and specialized knowledge is valuable. You never know what you might find or what idea might come to you. You will certainly start to become an expert in your area of research.

The process of researching and refining your idea is a natural part of changing your thought, your idea, into its money/energy making reality. It is part of a tried and true recipe for success.

If your initial research shows your idea is possible, then you must decide if you want to commit yourself to the project. If you do, you are on your way! The next step is to make a plan. A big plan

Decisions

New York City has countless theaters and many small shows are put on every day. The shows are fun, inexpensive (often free) for the audiences and good practice for up-and-coming actors. Occasionally someone asks a famous actor to be in one of these shows, and for whatever reason, he agrees to the gig.

At the height of his popularity, David Hyde Pierce, an actor most famous for playing the character Niles Crane on the television show *Frasier*, agreed to be in one of these small one-night-only shows. On the evening of the show, the lighting guy arrived early to the theater because he wanted to make sure everything worked perfectly that night. He entered what he thought would be a dark theater and was surprised to find a light on.

He looked up on the stage—and there was David Hyde Pierce! One of the world's most famous actors was on stage already rehearsing his lines for the small show! None of the other actors from the show were there, just a television star rehearsing his lines for that night's show. He certainly did not have to be there. If he had wanted to, he could have read his part from a paper script, and everyone would have still loved his performance.

However, years before David Hyde Pierce agreed to be in the small one-night show he *decided* to be one of the world's best actors. Once he decided his definite purpose, he took steps to make himself that which he had decided to be. Even after becoming one of the most famous people on television—he still was dedicated to being the best actor he could be. So much so that he went to the theater early to work on his lines, even for a "non-important" little show only a handful of people would see. This story shows the power of deciding what you want to do and who you want to be. It also shows you have to be "present" and working hard all the time, no matter how good you already are.

Decide and Take Action

Once you conduct your initial research and determine that your million-dollar idea is indeed viable, it is time for you to *decide* you will develop and execute the plan necessary to turn your idea into its reality.

The word "decide" comes from the Latin word *de-caedere*. This means "de-body" or to cut off. This is what you do when you decide to work on your idea. You cut off the possibility of not working on it—and you commit yourself to going forward to make the idea turn into a reality. That is, you commit to converting your thought energy (your idea) into its monetary equivalent (your million dollars).

If after your initial research you determine your idea is workable, you must decide quickly if you want to make your idea happen—and you must take immediate action to facilitate the process of transforming your million-dollar idea into reality.

This is a decisive moment for you and your idea. If you hesitate to take action on your viable idea, you risk never having a good idea again! Your subconscious, which worked so hard to give you your idea, may decide you are not serious about earning your million dollars. It may decide you are more serious about posting on Facebook, or watching television, or whatever it is you do with your precious time that is more important than bringing your million-dollar idea to the world.

You must take action immediately. You must work on developing your plan to make your idea a reality. You must put your plan down on paper and start thinking about everything you must do to make your idea real. Then, you must immediately take the first steps in your plan.

No Idling

Just as David Hyde Pierce works diligently on his acting, you must take steps to work on making your idea a reality. You must decide to do the work and then immediately start to *do* the work.

One of the world's most famous cello players informed an interviewer that even in his old age he still practiced four hours each day. The interviewer was surprised and asked the musician why he did this. "Because I am still getting better," came the reply. The cellist was so famous that he could easily rest on his laurels and simply perform at concerts. However, in his "off" time he was not idle. He practiced. He did the work.

Your million dollars waits for you. It is energy that already exists but has not yet come to you. It is yours, but it is waiting. To get it to come to you, you must take concrete steps— including taking the actions of creating and starting to execute a plan. These steps show your money you are serious about having it. It also moves you further down the path to having the money in your hands and bank account.

The Peril of Procrastination

"An idle mind is the devil's playground" says an old English proverb.

If you do not take action, you risk losing your chance. If you procrastinate and decide to first do something else, or save your idea until the perfect time, or wait until you have more money available, or any of a long list of other things—you run the risk of losing your million dollars. Money/energy is attracted to those that seek it, but it will not come to those that show they are not ready for it. Your level of energy, desire, and passion must match that of the energy represented by a million dollars.

Do you think the energy represented by one million dollars wants to sit and wait while you rest on a comfortable chair and watch a televised sporting event? Does the energy represented by one million dollars want to wait while you finish some other project that gives you some money/energy, but nothing that is close to one million dollars' worth of energy?

If your mind or hands are idle, if you are not actively pursuing your million dollars, it will not come to you. The devil or some other distraction, like Facebook or Instagram, will play in your idle mind and send you down a path that leads somewhere, anywhere, but not to your million dollars.

An idea can come and go as it pleases. Your million-dollar idea will come to you, but it can also go to someone else. If you sit idly and do not act upon your idea, it is possible someone else will do so.

An idea whose "time has come" cannot be stopped. Someone will act upon it. The energy of the idea is in the Universe and in the World—those that seek it can access it. In the United States, we know the inventors of the airplane are the Wright brothers. However, if you ask a Brazilian who invented the airplane, they will say Alberto Santos-Dumas. Dumas, a

Brazilian, flew an airplane publicly in Paris, France, a couple of years after the Wright brothers made their secretive and unknown flight.

Mr. Dumas was on another continent, but after eons without man flying, the time had come for the idea of human flight to be a reality. The Wright brothers and Dumas both acted upon the idea at about the same time in human history. The time had come, and man flew.

Has the time has come for your idea to be turned into a reality? If you want to earn your million dollars, you must decide the time has come.

A Not Blank Check

Many years before he became famous, the comedic actor Jim Carrey made a fateful decision one day in Hollywood. As he told Oprah Winfrey on her television show, he drove nightly into the Hollywood Hills overlooking Los Angeles, before he was famous, and envisioned producers telling him they liked his work. He could see and hear them talking to him, and they asked him to work for them. One night, he even decided to write himself a check for $10 million. He dated it for five years later, and in the memo section of the check, he wrote "for acting services rendered." He was giving himself five years to get paid $10 million.

Mr. Carrey *decided* he wanted to be paid millions for acting. He put this thought down on paper and kept it in his wallet to remind himself of his end goal. He made a conscious decision that he would be successful. He saw that reminder in his wallet countless times... and it influenced thoughts in his subconscious.

While "daydreaming," he imagined himself in possession of many valuable items; his thinking was as if he already had the items. "Well," he said to Oprah, "they were my items, but I just didn't have them in my hands yet." He had already decided he was rich—in his imagination/head he had many of the things he would have when he was rich. So, he was already living that life or, at least, thinking that he was living life with a million dollars.

Five years later, Mr. Carrey, right before Thanksgiving, received word that he had come to terms with a movie production company for a picture called *Dumb and Dumber*. For making the movie, he would be paid ten million dollars.

Do you think it was a pure coincidence that he was paid exactly $10 million "for acting services rendered?" No! This was the exact amount he decided to earn when he wrote the check to himself in the Hollywood Hills. By reading more of this book, you will come to realize it was not at all a coincidence. He put that amount into his head (and on paper into his wallet) and the Universe delivered to him that exact amount!

A Woman at her Kitchen Table

In 2000, a woman in New York City was tired of the "rat race" she was living in while working at magazine company. She decided to quit her job to start an online email company. It was a major step, and the decision changed her life forever.

The simple beginning of Dany Levy's (soon to be million-dollar) business took place at her kitchen table in an apartment in New York City's West Village. There, she sent out a single email to her contact list of 700 email addresses. The next day, she sent another single email. The emails told recipients what they needed to know or do that day in NYC. The emails were well received, and people began to ask to be included on the email list. The size of the email list grew.

One day her phone rang, and it was a company asking if they could advertise in her daily email. She had not asked for advertisers—someone actually came to her and said they wanted to give her money! The advertiser asked what it would cost, and Ms. Levy made a dollar number up on the spot. The advertiser agreed, and she had her first sale.

In three years, her *Daily Candy* email list grew to over 200,000 subscribers. Then, she sold a portion of her company for $3 million, and in 2008, the entire company sold for $125 million.

All of these millions of dollars stemmed from her simple decision to make a change—to cut herself off from the big corporate magazine world in which she was living and to work on her own million-dollar idea. Had she stayed at her old job she never would have made her millions. Her idea combined with her decision to take action led her to her million dollars.

Your Power to Decide

The power to make a million dollars is in your hands. It is in your brain. You have the power to decide to no longer live without your million dollars. Just like any person—an actor, a magazine worker—you can decide to take control of your monetary and life situation.

First, you must decide you are ready for it. Then, you must come up with your idea. Next, you must decide to develop and work on your plan. In these ways your million dollars knows it can come to you. Let it!

Look at the similarities between what Jim Carrey discussed with Oprah and the steps covered in this book. Look carefully at the parallels between the *process* described in this book and the *actions* he took.

Does it need to be made clearer to you?

The good news is that you are now on the right path. You decided to spend some of your energy reading this book. Next, you must decide that you will do what it suggests—and write yourself your own check!

Millions Using Technology

M any men make fortunes leveraging technological advances. Facebook and Google made billions of dollars for their founders. The CEOs of Airbnb and Uber are also extraordinarily wealthy.

There are many non-technological ways to make millions of dollars. However, since many millionaires used or exploited technology to make millions, it is useful to examine their success. Read the stories to see how these men used technology to make money. It may give you ideas on how you can use or leverage technology to make your millions.

While the recent stories of Facebook, Google, etc. are good examples of how to make money using technology, our current era is not the first time this has happened. History has many examples when men used technology to make millions of dollars.

Technology in History

In the early 1930s, the U.S. Defense Department invented a type of reverse sonar-related machine. It did not listen for sounds like a radar, but instead generated different and new sounds. The first person who bought one of these machines was a man using new technologies for entertainment. His name was Walt Disney. The sounds he incorporated into his "talking" movies enthralled the world. He profited greatly from it.

In the 1950s, a petroleum company invented a new plastic. Two men at a toy company used the new technology to manufacture a simple plastic hoop. After a bit of marketing, the "Hula Hoop" sold twenty-five million units in four months and one hundred million in two years.

In 1994, a man with a Wall Street finance background surveyed the new technological world known then as the "World Wide Web." He thought it was the wave of the future and pondered what kind of business could benefit from its use. He decided a giant bookstore was the best idea. He was right. This is how Jeff Bezos started Amazon. Now he employees over 30,000 people. His company is worth over $800 billion. His share is worth $170 billion.

Mark Cuban's first job after earning a management degree was bartending. Then, he was a salesclerk for a software shop. Subsequently, he started his own business-computer-and-software company. When he sold it seven years later, he netted $2 million. He made his first million in technology without having a technology background.

Cuban's serious money came from his next venture, which he did not start. Two men started a company to transmit audio broadcasts of sporting events on the new platform called the Internet. They convinced Cuban to run the company, Broadcast.com. He made $300 million when it sold to Yahoo!. (And to show you how this man thinks, he is now trying to do the same thing again—except this time the broadcasts include video.)

In the "slums" up in the hills above Rio de Janeiro, Brazil, one man realized his friends all had motor scooters and cell phones. He positioned himself as a middleman/agent and started a food delivery service. He leveraged existing technology, at no cost to him, to develop a successful business. He did not make a million dollars in this business, but he made a lot of money in a dirt-poor section of Brazil.

Technology for Non-technical People

You do not have to be a hard-core programmer, computer scientist, or technical expert like the Facebook or Google founders to make your million dollars. There are plenty of opportunities to make your million dollars in technology that do not require strong technical knowledge. It is possible to leave the details to technology experts and still reap benefits from advancements in technology.

Steve Jobs founded Apple Computer. However, the technical genius of the company was Steve Wozniak. Jobs asked Wozniak if certain things were technologically possible to build. When Wozniak said yes, Jobs went out and sold the new technology.

Jobs visited Xerox PARC, a research center in Silicon Valley, and saw new technology on display. He realized he could incorporate the technology into his new computers, so he "stole" those ideas and sold them in his new machines. The Macintosh computer incorporated a graphical screen and a "mouse"; Xerox PARC invented them, not Apple Inc.

This example shows that the genius of Steve Jobs was not his initial technological knowledge, but rather his ability to see what could be done and what needed to be done with new technology. That combined with a strong drive to force things to happen to his liking made Apple the wildly successful company that it is.

As for your author, I used existing technology to create something new: a handheld GPS tour guide. The hardware was not new, but the way I employed it and the "system and method" which I implemented was new. I do have some computer programming skills, but it would have been completely possible to create this new invention without having these skills.

Jobs was not a programmer but created the world's largest computer company. Disney was not a sonar expert but realized the machines would help him create sounds he could use in his new movies. In all of these examples, someone was able to leverage new technology to make themselves millions of dollars. You can do the same—even if you are not a technology expert.

A Seeking Man Sells Hamburgers

Advancements in technology create opportunities for people who are seeking opportunities. One thing the men in these examples all have in common is that they were all looking for ways to improve life using relatively new technology. If you are going to make your million in technology, you need to be on the lookout for opportunities.

Ray Kroc is famous for inventing the McDonald's hamburger chain. However, it might surprise you to learn he did *not* invent McDonald's. The man who made a fortune from "McDonald's" was first a failing ice cream/malt machine salesman. Another company had better technology, and his sales were hurt because of it. He knew he was in trouble and needed to make a change.

In 1954, a restaurant in California placed a large order with him—which surprised him so much he went to California to visit the place. As he traveled across the country, he did not know his life was about to change forever.

In San Bernardino, Kroc saw a new restaurant with a speedy hamburger delivery system. It was perfect for delivering hamburgers to Americans who were, at the time, falling in love with their new automobiles. A hardworking salesman, Kroc had seen countless kitchens across the country. He realized that this restaurant's technology/process was new and special.

He convinced the McDonald brothers to let him sell franchises of their restaurant. He was wildly successful and amassed a fortune of $600 million. The McDonald brothers sold everything to Kroc seven years after meeting him, netting $1 million each.

Kroc did not invent the new system of making and delivering hamburgers, the McDonald brothers did. But Kroc saw a way to use this new system and built one of the most successful businesses in the world. All of this happened because he knew he had to make a change—and he was actively looking for opportunities.

What About You?

To make your million dollars you will do the same thing. You will put your mind into a state where it is always actively seeking and looking for new ideas. The section of this book discussing your "incantation" helps you with this. Once you focus your brain on seeing opportunities and ways to improve things, you will start to see the opportunities that are in front of you.

It does not take a technical expert to make money in technology. The technology world is constantly inventing new things and creating new opportunities. The opportunities are out there—waiting for someone who is looking for them.

Technical Specifics

Once you have your technical idea, you need to learn everything you can in that area. The more you know, the easier it will be to work with the experts in the field as they do their work for you. You will want to read technical documentations for your technology. The information you want to know is in the user guides and technical specification documents for the technology, not the glossy brochures provided by marketing departments.

In my case, I found an online copy of the original top-secret plans for the U.S. Global Positioning Satellite system. Lockheed and Martin Marietta, the top two aerospace companies in the U.S., produced the document jointly. While the declassified document was redacted, it was fascinating to see the source document for one of the most advanced technological achievements in the history of mankind. Reading this document helped me understand how the system works and made me more comfortable and confident when I discussed it with other people.

By reading and learning as much as you can about technical aspects of your project, you greatly increase your chances of success. You might not be a complete expert on the topic, but at least you are somewhat of an expert and can ask good, "educated" questions when needed. This is what Steve Jobs could do. In this manner, a non-technical person can prosper in technology.

Leadership and Planning

On September 11, 2001, terrorists hijacked four airplanes in the United States. They used them to kill nearly 3,000 people and destroy several buildings. One man stepped up to lead New York City and the nation through one of the biggest crises in the history of the country. His name was Rudy Giuliani, and he was the mayor of New York City.

The fact that he was able to lead the city and the nation at that critical time was not a surprise. As with any good leader, he planned and prepared for anything he could think of, including this type of emergency. He and his staff had rehearsed and drilled for this type of situation. That is why, when this terrible event occurred, he was ready. He executed his plan.

His planning, preparation, and diligence was evident on his first day as mayor. After the election but before he was sworn in as the mayor, he spent his time reading the entire code of New York City. On his first day in office he knew all of the laws, rules, and regulations pertaining to the city. When union leaders and others tried to influence his decisions—and tried to tell him what the laws said, he replied that he knew what the laws said because he had just read them all. He was prepared.

In your quest for your million dollars you must be as prepared and thorough as Mayor Giuliani. You must develop plans, develop contingencies, and you must know everything you can about your product, service, or idea. You must be ready for anything. Then, you must be the leader who executes the plan that yields your million dollars.

Nobody else is going to do this work for you. It is up to *you*. It is your idea, and your time has come to execute a plan to deliver on the idea. To do so, you must develop a plan that encompasses everything you need to do to successfully implement your idea and earn your million dollars.

It will take you time to develop this plan—and you will likely add and change portions of it over time. However, the plan is vital to your success. In addition, the planning process itself will be very useful to you. When you develop your plan, you will certainly think of things you had not thought of as necessary before. You will realize there are many contingencies involved—and a sequence of required events will unfold once you have delineated the steps required of you to achieve your success.

Your Plan

Different people have different methods for developing plans. I recommend simply sitting somewhere quiet with a notebook or paper and writing down everything you can think of that you need to do. You will think of many things, and they will come to you a bit "randomly." Write them all down. Once you have your large list you can organize them and determine what needs to be done first, second, and so on.

In addition to listing everything you need to do, you must estimate how much time is required for each step. Develop an overall time line that shows how long it will be until you are ready to launch your product, service, or idea. It shows you the key milestones you must hit along the way to keep yourself on the path to success.

While developing your timeline you will realize how much money you need to fund your idea and when you will need it. Do you need money to buy materials? Rent buildings? Pay for advertising? Pay for software? Pay employees? Pay contractors? Keep track of this information because you, as the leader, must be prepared to pay for whatever is necessary in order to make your plan happen.

Once your plan solidifies, you can transfer your notes to a computer. An organized version of your plan will help you keep track of everything you need to do. A simple project-planning software program will make your plan look better.

A "presentable" plan is also useful for communicating with other people. When you share your ideas and vision with potential coworkers, you can show them your plan. The simple fact that you took the time to lay everything out on paper will help show them how serious you are about your plans. It will also help them see your vision since the steps involved are laid out in front of them.

The same can be said if you need financial assistance to help you reach your million dollars. Loan managers at banks and venture capitalists all want to see well-thought-out plans—in part to determine if your idea will work—and in part to see how serious you are about your endeavor. Showing up with printouts from Microsoft Project or other planning software helps establish your credibility.

Planning for an Important Meeting

A common mistake of unsuccessful businesspeople is to show up for a meeting unprepared. Good businessmen, and especially good salesmen, prepare for their meetings.

The more important the meeting, the more time you should spend preparing for it.

Before the meeting, decide what is its purpose and objective. You need to have an end goal in mind and work towards it during the meeting. The purpose of the meeting may be to describe your idea/business/product/service and its benefits. The objective may be to get agreement that you should send a contract to your potential customer. Many times, people enter meetings without knowing why, exactly, they are there. This will waste people's time—and it is up to you (filled with passion, desire, and having a great idea) to make the meeting worthwhile.

You should "rehearse" the meeting in your head and with your team (if they will join you in the meeting). Think about what questions might come up during the meeting. What objections might people have to signing on with your idea? What will you do if the projector breaks? Or your computer malfunctions?

Immediately prior to an important meeting, you may want to raise your energy level. Accomplish this with coffee, loud music, or in whatever manner you choose.

My Story—Planning and Product Development

In the case of the GPS tour guide system, my plan established two broad areas of development: product and marketing. I needed to develop my product and I needed to develop a way to market and sell the product.

The original planning for the product showed I needed to do many things, including:

- Developing a list of "points-of-interest (POIs)" in New York City
- Develop a database of latitudes and longitudes for those POIs
- Develop a tour guide script for each POI
- Record the audio (and/or video) files for each POI
- Collect historical photos and videos for use in the system
- Develop the software to be used by tourists
    o Develop software specifications
    o Find and hire programmer
    o Work with programmer to develop application
- Research and purchase hardware (computers, GPS receivers, lanyards, etc.)
- Research and purchase software (map software, GPS splitting utility)
- Test the software
- Make any required changes
- Beta test the system with actual users

Later I added:

- Develop list of locations of NYC subway stations most used by tourists
- Develop list of locations of "public" restrooms in NYC
- Develop latitude/longitude database for these locations
- Add these to the system

Out of all of these items, the only one with which I had much difficulty was finding a computer programmer who could handle the job. The other items were straightforward, although completing the tasks took considerable time.

For script development, I wandered the streets of NYC to make sure I knew what a tourist would see and ask about. For historical photos, I scoured the Internet and found public-use photos that showed old views of NYC streets and landmarks. I already knew the locations of the subway stations, so I used Google Maps to find their latitudes and longitudes.

For the latitudes and longitudes of most of the other 300 points-of-interest, I used Microsoft Excel to create a small spreadsheet. This database included descriptions of the POIs as well as their street addresses. Rather than spend hours looking up each POI on Google Maps, I found an online service that converted street addresses to latitudes and longitudes. I paid $50 for the service and saved many hours of work.

Finding the programmer to help with the application took some time. Initially I posted an advertisement on the Silicon Valley version of Craigslist, seeking help with my program. At the time, cell phones did not have GPS capability and not many programmers had experience with GPS. I knew that if anyone could do the project they would likely be in Silicon Valley.

Sure enough, I received several responses. However, only a few of them had experience that showed me they might be able to do the job. Then I received the perfect resume. The programmer already had experience with a GPS tour guide system! In fact, it was the guy who wrote the program for the Go Car system in San Francisco! We talked on the phone— but mutually agreed he could not do the work for me due to a possible conflict of interest.

Eventually I ran out of candidates, and I had not found someone who I was certain could do the job. I continued working on other items from the plan but knew I had to find someone to write the program. A month passed, and I needed a solution. Then one day I thought, "Where else do they have really technical computer programmers?" I remembered the Massachusetts Institute of Technology, or MIT. For a few years I lived just down the street from the school. They have some of the best programmers in the world.

Someone I know graduated from MIT, so I emailed him and asked if the school had any type of online job board. He said yes and posted an ad for me. Two hours later, I was talking to one of the best programmers in the world. He was, of course, located in Silicon Valley. He said that for a healthy fee he could write my program. This solved my problem.

Once I had a programmer, I felt good about my product development plan. I was confident I had thought of everything I needed to develop the product, and all I had to do was execute the steps in the plan. I knew when all of the items were complete we would combine the assets and have the world's first handheld GPS tour guide system.

Marketing and Selling

The plan for marketing and selling the system was not as clear. I knew I would need several things including:

- A full marketing plan (listing when, where, and how I would advertise and/or market my product)
- A website
- A media kit
- Press releases
- An intriguing company logo
- Text to describe the GPS tour guide system
- Media-ready photos and video ("B-roll")

What I was not sure about was how to do the actual selling. (See marketing section of this book). So, at the initial stages of development I had a plan to make a plan. I knew the product was new and was not sure what would be the best way to sell it. I knew I had to make a plan to test different methods of marketing, advertising, and selling to see what would work.

Leadership

Every step in the plans above was my responsibility. If I did not make these things happen, my idea and product would be useless. I delegated many things (e.g., hired a programmer, hired a website developer), but I kept in contact with them so I knew progress was happening. If any of the plan items did not happen, my plan would fail. As a leader, this was not acceptable and was not going to happen.

To make your million dollars, *you* must develop a sound plan and make sure it is executed perfectly. You are responsible for this, not anyone else. Then, you must work very hard to give yourself the maximum chance of success.

Added Power

———————◆———————

At some point after practicing your focused incantation, you will receive your million-dollar idea. It will hit you like a soft bolt of lightning, and you will be very excited. Once the initial excitement has subsided a bit, you will realize you tapped into an infinitely powerful energy source, and it gave you the idea. The enormity of the energy source and its power is staggering.

You will follow up on your idea with initial research to see if it is feasible to execute your idea. Then, you will create a plan with which to develop your idea and change it from an idea into reality. This is the path to your million dollars.

However, your plan is useless if you are powerless to make it happen. If you lack the desire or drive to execute your plan or think you do not have the resources to make it happen, your plan will never come to fruition. This book has already discussed desire and faith as required elements on your way to your million dollars. This section discusses the power required to execute your plan.

Once you have your plan, it is time to tap into an additional power source. It is not the same source you tapped into to receive your idea (although that source is always available to you when needed). You will not be able to execute your plan without additional power, knowledge, and energy.

You need the assistance and participation of other people. Other people have additional energy you need to convert your idea into a million dollars. Other people have knowledge and experience you need. Other people have contacts and connections you need. There is a wealth of useful power, information, and energy stored in other people. You can tap into it and bring it out to make your plan happen.

The good news is that under the right conditions and circumstances other people will be happy to work with you to help you with your vision. Many people go through their lives working on something that is un-challenging or boring to them. The opportunity you bring them is to work on a new interesting idea, on a well-thought-out plan. These things will appeal to them.

It is an opportunity for them to work with other good people that you are bringing together for the purpose of executing your plan and developing your idea. By being part of this group, they will experience something more interesting, intriguing, valuable, and fulfilling than if they did not work with you and your group.

Compensation

It is your job as leader to develop the team required to execute your plan. You will need to show group members your plan and have them understand your vision as well as their role in your organization. They will also need to understand the compensation they will receive for their participation.

Nobody will work for long on any project without adequate compensation. Monetary payment for their time is easiest way to acquire someone's cooperation, assuming you have the money to pay them. However, do not underestimate the value of being a part of a good team and participating in something new. Many people like to create—and being able to help create a new business is exciting.

If your idea is exciting, you will find some people will do at least some work for you free of charge. People do not always require payment with money for the work that they do.

Some people you need in your group may want to become part owners of your company. You will have to determine the value of their participation compared to what percentage of your company they request to own.

The Power of Group Synergy

When you put together your group, something akin to magic happens. First, you can utilize and leverage the knowledge, time, and energy of the new members. You know your plan better than anyone does, but the people in your group know things you do not know. By bringing them into your group, you increase the power of the group and the power of everyone in the group. You have more power and are able to accomplish much more.

Author Napoleon Hill discussed this power in the 1930s. More recently, author/speaker Steven Johnson gave a TED Talk answering the question, "Where (do) good ideas come from?" The answer, according to recent research, is "from within groups."

Groups benefit from "synergy." The power of combining different people truly is greater than the sum of the talents of the individual group members. In-group discussions of the ideas and information given by various members combine to yield new thoughts and ideas that would not exist had the group not gotten together. When a group gathers to think about and work on a definite purpose, an added energy develops that does not exist if each group member is working alone.

Individual skill sets are of limited value compared to what they can be used to accomplish when combined in a group. For a simple example, simply look at men who know the skills of carpentry, plumbing, bricklaying, electrical wiring, and glass creating. Individually they can only do so much, but put them into a group with a sound blueprint or plan and they build a house. Combining skills creates things of great value.

As a leader, you provide the plan or blueprint. You gather the group with a definite plan and purpose in mind. You leverage power from multiple sources, provide a plan, and create something of value.

If you examine the history of men who have made millions, you will see most of them used the power of a strong group to accomplish their goals. The men leverage the power and energy found in other people and benefit from the energy and power of group synergy. These two sources of energy are available to you. They will help you acquire your million dollars.

My Story

The plan for my GPS tour guide system required product development followed by marketing and sales.

For product development, I combined the talents of voice-over artists, a sound engineer, and computer programmers. I combined historic and other information from many different sources into an up-to-date tour script. Each person and source added his or her own ideas and talents to the product development process. I was able to define exactly what was needed from each group member, but inevitably each member added things from their background and experience that helped the project beyond my delineation. The result was a fantastic never-before-experienced tour guide system.

Finding Resources

You will have to find the resources you need to help you. Spend plenty of time on this, and get the best people you can find.

In my case, since I was in New York City, it was easy to find actors with very good voices to record the tour guide material. Next, the sound engineer did a great job and produced a much better product than if I had tried to record the material myself. His knowledge of digital editing tools was very helpful, especially when we had to record versions of a special tour in five different languages. He also added sound effects, music, and other voices to the system—which made the final product one of the best in the world.

You must hire workers who have expertise in what you require. The quality of sound for my GPS tour guide system was far superior to tour guide systems that recorded their sound using untrained people to narrate the tour. Everyone thinks they can read a script and record it. If they do, the result is not as good as having a professional do the work. Your million-dollar idea might not require you to record audio files, but there may be similar tasks that could benefit from having professionals do the work. Take advantage of them in order to make a better product or service.

I used the Craigslist website to hire voice-over artists and workers for my rental stands. The sound engineer I knew from a previous project, but I also originally found him using Craigslist.

It was helpful to be in NYC where the actors are located, but thanks to the Internet, it is possible to find talent and specialized knowledge in other parts of the world and use them for your project.

If you need actors, look for talent in Los Angeles and New York City. If you need agricultural knowledge, look to Iowa. If you have a new device for downhill skiing, you can find knowledgeable people in Colorado. There is always a resource available somewhere with information and/or energy you can use to help advance your plan. The Internet provides a way to find these people whether you are in the United States or another country.

Some million-dollar ideas are possible only because of the opportunities the Internet creates. I knew the programmer I needed was likely to be in Silicon Valley—and the Internet allowed me to find him without being anywhere near Palo Alto, California. Somewhat similarly, there might not be a market for your product where you live, but the Internet allows you to sell to anyone anywhere in the world.

Power

Whether you find your group members online or in your backyard, creating a group and working with other people are required for you to acquire your million dollars. By tapping into this power source, you are leveraging the energy and knowledge of individuals in order to create something of value.

This process has been used throughout time to create much of the wealth that man enjoys. From the pyramids in Egypt and Mexico to today's amazing capability to fly nonstop to anywhere in the world, these valuable and beautiful things all started as ideas in someone's brain. The ideas led to plans, and groups formed to accomplish the plans. Through that process, the ideas, the energy of thoughts, were changed into things of value.

To earn your million dollars, you need your idea, your plans, and the power available to you from other people. That power is leveraged in a group. This is the how millions are earned. This is how you will earn your million dollars.

Marketing

M arketing is everything you do to get the word out about your product or service. Selling is not part of marketing but can be an opportunity for further marketing. Obviously, making the sale is more important than marketing, but usually you need to execute solid marketing before you make many sales.

If you do not know a lot about marketing, you will need to learn about branding, positioning, advertising, and publicity (see chapter on "How to Obtain Free Publicity"). You will also need a memorized "elevator pitch." (See howtomakeamillion. com for book and other resource recommendations.)

I have some knowledge to supplant the information found in other sources. First, if you are only going to do one thing— then do not do anything. Doing just one thing is a waste of time. Marketing needs reinforcement as your customer gets used to the idea of making his first purchase from you.

Although it is possible, do not expect a single effort to yield much in the way of results. Again, it depends in part on your million-dollar idea. What is appropriate for you to do depends on your million-dollar idea. What works for one product or service might not work for another.

You will need to examine the "marketing landscape" and decide what is appropriate for your efforts. The term "marketing landscape" simply means what your competition and similar industry competition is doing.

When it comes time to develop and execute your initial marketing plan—what you need to do depends on your product or service. If you do something similar to what someone else has already done, then you can study what they did to market and sell their products. If you are doing something completely novel, then you will not have a clear guide as to what will work for you. You will have to try different things and determine which work the best for you.

Copy Someone

If your product or service is similar to another well-established business, it may be possible to copy their advertising approach. Where do you see advertisements for their business? Do they run the ads regularly? If they do, it means they think it is working for them. You might want to do the same thing. This approach could help you spend your investment money more efficiently.

Most importantly, make sure you have everything ready to go before you let the public know about your product or service. If you happen to have a huge marketing and sales success, you do not want your new customers to be disappointed due to your lack of preparation and readiness.

Be Original

On the other hand, taking a novel approach to marketing can be extremely beneficial. The Dollar Shave Club did that when they started their business.

The Dollar Shave Club sells cheap razor blades on a subscription basis. To start marketing their service, they made a very funny and original advertisement showing the CEO walking through their factory and talking about the service. They posted the funny advertisement on the Internet. Millions of people shared it with their friends. The company received a huge amount of publicity at no additional cost.

Their initial success was so great that they had to apologize to their new customers for delivery delays due to lack of available razor blades! Again, they did this in a funny manner, keeping with the "look and feel" of the brand image found in their initial advertisement.

Their product launch had great success followed by productions problems. However, the end of their story is impressive—five years later the company sold to industry giant Unilever for $1 billion.

Prior to Product or Service Launch

Whether you copy someone else's approach or go with original ideas, there are several things to consider before launching your product or service. These are among the possible items you should consider:

- What do you want your "brand" to represent? What is the "look and feel" of your business?
- Website (As with other elements of your marketing, it should incorporate your chosen "look and feel.")

- Email campaign (A series of emails ready to send to your potential customers. They must provide value or nobody will want to receive them.)
- How will you get press coverage? (TV? Radio? Blogs? Magazine stories?)
- Product or service descriptions and "selling" points
- Benefits list for the consumer
- How-to videos, demonstration and/or showcase videos
- Company "B-roll" videos (short video clips ready for publicity or use on TV and the Internet)
- Press kit, press releases
- Lists of potential customers (data file)
- Do you want or need Facebook, Twitter, or Instagram (etc.) accounts?

This list is certainly not complete. What is appropriate for you depends on your million-dollar idea. Items not listed here might be more valuable to you.

The Basics of Who and Why

The questions you will need to answer along the way in the development of your marketing plan include the following:

Who will buy your product?

Why will they buy your product?

Where do you find these people?

What do these people do?

What media do they use? (What media channels: TV, radio, Internet, etc.,—and which locations: which TV/ Radio shows, which sections of which newspapers, etc.?)

The bottom line on marketing is that you must do whatever it takes to get the word out about your product and to create sales. For some ideas this will be easy; for others it will require more effort. It will require consideration of the items discussed here and more. You must do whatever it takes, but you will have your faith and desire to push you forward.

My Story

Marketing and selling a brand-new technology device to tourists in New York City presented some unique challenges. The product was new, so tourists coming to the city knew nothing about the product.

I decided to focus marketing on two areas:

- Getting publicity via newspapers, magazines, and radio
- Semi-direct selling to tourists via concierge services at hotels

We also tested advertising in tourist magazines and placing a rental desk in the lobby of a tourist hotel. None of the methods worked as well I wanted them to work.

Website

I had enough skill to put up a simple website but decided to hire someone to develop the web site, logo, and color scheme for

"CityShow NYC—The World's Coolest GPS Tour Guide." A referral from a trusted source did great work. This move freed up some of my time since I knew the website development was in capable hands.

Once I had the website operating, I initiated work on other aspects of marketing. I knew if I talked to a hotel concierge, he would ask to see a website for the product. So that was the first item of my marketing campaign.

NYC Hotel Concierges

I had the great fortune of finding an Excel file containing an email list of the directors at all the hotels in New York City (I describe how I got this file later in this chapter). I wanted the concierges to act as sales agents for the GPS tour guide, so I sent an email to the directors of the hotels.

The email was "positioned" (a marketing term) as a press release, but I did not send it to the press, only to the hotel directors. I worked hard on getting the wording of the email just right. Then I spent a lot of time on the "subject" line of the email to maximize the chance that a director would open and read the email. I settled on something along the lines of "World Debut of NYC's new GPS Tour Guide System to be held at Your Hotel?"

I sent the email to approximately 100 hotels. Within two days I received responses from five of them. The responders included the Radisson, the five-star NY Palace, and W Times Square. Each of these places has a different clientele, which was good. That way I could see if the device resonated better with any specific type of tourist.

I met with whoever was willing to meet. I started with a small hotel, in case I was nervous and made a mistake in my presentation. This was a good strategy, as I was a little nervous in the first meeting. The subsequent meetings were much easier.

Concierges at three of the hotels agreed to take devices and try to rent them. The price was $49 per day—to split between my company and the concierge. I did not know if that was a fair deal, but at this point I was more interested in generating my first sales via concierges than I was in making money.

I delivered a few devices to each concierge and told them I could get more to them if needed. I showed them how to work the device and how to keep its battery charged. Then I left and crossed my fingers that we would rent some devices to tourists using this method.

I checked back in at each of the hotels a day or two later. There were no rentals. This was not good news, but I knew there was still time. However, after two weeks there had been no rentals, and I knew the batteries were possibly dead. The concierge experiment had failed.

What I learned from this experience was that hotel concierges are reactive to their guest's wishes. They want to the guest to be happy, so they help with dinner reservations or tickets to a show if the guest asks about these things. A concierge does not want to explain a new GPS device to a tourist, and they do not want to try to "sell" anything. If a guest had asked about the device, the concierge would have delivered it to them. However, since the device was brand new nobody was asking about it—so no rentals.

Surprisingly, the concierge route failed to produce *any* rentals. It was a sad experience to go to the concierge desks and pick up the devices, which inevitably had low batteries, but you have to be prepared for "failures" along the path to a million dollars.

NYC Hotel

We had a rental desk in the lobby of an NYC hotel.

Somehow, I met the wonderful woman who runs the Wellington Hotel on the corner of 7th Avenue and 55th Street. It is a clean tourist hotel in a great location (with small rooms and high prices, like all NYC hotels). Out of the kindness of her heart (people will help you if you have a good idea and need help), she allowed me to set up a rental desk in the lobby of her hotel. She also allowed me to place advertisements for the device (a postcard in a standing plastic frame) in all her hotel rooms. She did not charge anything or ask for anything in exchange for this help. However, I added the hotel to the points-of-interest on the GPS tour guide system as a thank-you gesture and as a little "free advertising" for the hotel.

I staffed the rental booth (with someone who is now a famous television and Broadway actress) and tried the experiment for a week. This was plenty of time since many tourists are in NYC for only a few days. Our test would cover at least two hotel's worth of tourists. The experiment failed. There were no rentals from this approach, and it was clear the economics would not work. Paying the rental desk attendant required that we rented at least two devices a day just to break even. That did not happen.

Tourist Magazine

Later, we advertised in a weekly NYC tourist magazine. At first. we tried a small advertisement but did not see more than one or two sales from the ad. I tried a larger advertisement, but it had the same disappointing result. The only good news was that at the time we were operating the special Top of the Rock version of the tour and had a rental desk inside Rockefeller

Center. The ad listed our location (as did our website), and the tourists could rent and pick up their device from that location. From a logistical standpoint this worked well.

Press Release

The one aspect of our marketing that had the intended effect was a press release. The press release announced the world debut of a GPS tour guide system in NYC. The press release garnered us an article in the *New York Times* and mentions from *National Geographic*, *The Economist*, and several other magazines. *National Geographic* even had someone rent one the devices.

Discussion of press releases and related items is in the chapter, "How to Obtain Free Publicity."

Other Efforts & an Accidental Gift

When it was time to get serious about marketing and selling or renting my "World's Coolest GPS Tour Guide," I did not know the best way to rent the devices to tourists.

I had several questions: Did I need a rental stand that they could visit? Should I deliver the devices to their hotel rooms? Could I enlist the concierge desks of the main tourist hotels to either talk up or directly rent my devices to tourists?

My attention was on these questions when one day I heard an advertisement on a taxi's radio. Usually I take the subway in NYC, but for some reason I was in a taxi. The advertisement touted the country's largest hotel and tourist convention. It started the next day at NYC's Javits convention center. "Oh," I thought, "If anyone would know something about tourists in NYC it would be the people at that convention."

The next day I took the subway up to Midtown and walked across Manhattan to the convention center next to the Hudson River. I did not have a plan *at all*, other than to see what was going on. I really did not know for certain why I was going to the event, but something told me it was a good idea.

Inside the building, tickets were on sale for entrance into the main exhibit hall. The tickets were expensive. But before I bought a ticket, out in the lobby I saw a company booth with a banner that said the people were from the NYC hotel association. I thought that might be a good place to start.

I approached the booth and asked if they might help me. I explained I had invented the world's first handheld GPS tour guide and was trying to figure out how to best rent it to tourists in NYC.

This was the first time I had told anyone in public about my new invention. "Oh, that's cool!" the woman said. It was the first of many positive responses regarding the device. "I am not sure what you should do, but you should probably come to our annual meeting tonight. Someone there will know what you should do!"

Just like that, I was invited into the world of New York City hotels and tourism. I told the woman I would certainly attend and thanked her for the invitation.

I wandered around the lobby a bit more but decided not to pay the money to enter the main hall. It was an international exhibition and my product was (for now) only useful in New York. Instead, I decided to go home and research the NYC hotel organization.

I poked around on the organization's website. The group consisted of all the hotels in New York City. Their concerns included things such as the building of other hotels in New York City, general tourism numbers, the NYC tourist-and-convention bureau, etc.

The group was straightforward, and the website was mostly uninteresting. However, I found a very interesting file. It contained the contact list of the entire membership. Most importantly to me, it contained the email addresses of everyone in the group! I could not believe my luck. What a gift to find! I wanted to contact the general managers of each hotel in NYC, and I had just found a list with all of their names and email addresses!

This book discusses desire and faith as the main tenants required for you to earn your million dollars. I have no doubt this email address list came to me because of my desire, focus, passion, and the work I had done to date. It was exactly what I needed, and it came to me out of nowhere.

Had I not been in the taxi, I would not have heard the advertisement for the convention. Had I not decided to go, I would never have found the hotel association's booth. If I had not done that, I would not have been invited to their annual meeting. As it turned out, these things were very important to my business.

If you do not have a clear marketing plan, you will need to try different things to see what might work for you. You will not always know which things will work and what will not work. So, you must do as many things as you can try to see what works for you. I did not know exactly why I went to the hotel convention, but I went anyway. I knew there might be something or someone useful there, so I went. It paid off for me.

Your Elevator Pitch

I visited the convention center during the day. That same night I went to the annual NYC hotel meeting. It is the one night of the year representatives from every hotel in New York City get together to discuss business. On this night, the main topic was "What are we going to do about Airbnb, the website that allows people to rent their apartments to visitors, which takes away money from us!"

After the main meeting there was a cocktail party. I talked to several people. When they asked, "What do you do?" I told them about my GPS tour guide. "Oh, you should talk to Christine!" said four different people.

Later, another person at the party told me I should talk to Christine. Then he added, "And there she is!", as he pointed at a woman heading to the exit while putting on her coat. Christine was the woman who ran the NYC tourist-and-convention bureau. Not surprisingly, this is a huge and important organization in NYC.

I knew I had to act immediately. I jumped out of my chair and strode over towards her. I took the biggest steps I could to get there as soon as possible, but I did not want to run towards her as that would look ridiculous.

When I reached her I said, "Hello Christine! I just had four people tell me I should talk to you. My name is Brian Teasley, and I have something I think you might really like."

"Really?" she said. "Ok..."

"I have invented the world's first handheld GPS tour guide. You walk around Manhattan, it knows where you are, and it tells you things."

Her reaction was positive. She reached into her purse, took out her business card and said, "Here's my card. Give me a call on Monday, and we will set up a meeting."

The total time of this "meeting" was about one minute. The value was immense. I had just met and obtained a meeting with the most well-known and best-connected tourism expert in the world. Not bad for a sixty-second meeting. However, there was more time spent in preparation for this sixty-second meeting than sixty seconds.

The key to this successful sixty-second meeting was that I was ready for it. I had spent at least an hour or two constructing the three important sentences I said to her:

"I have something you are really going to like. I have invented the world's first handheld GPS tour guide. You walk around Manhattan, it knows where you are, and it tells you things."

That was (and still is) my elevator pitch.

The elevator pitch is something you prepare ahead of time to deliver to people who inquire about your product, service, or idea. You never know who you might meet and under what circumstance. You might be in an elevator and in comes somebody who has something you want or need for your million-dollar idea or for your team. You only have a very short time to deliver your message, so every word counts.

In my case, I had rehearsed these lines repeatedly. When it came time to deliver these lines to one of the most connected people in the world, the words came out smoothly and easily. I did not waste any of her time (something you quickly learn not to do in New York City). I told her exactly what I was "selling" and painted a picture in her head of how it would work for someone using the GPS tour guide in Manhattan.

Whatever you choose for your million-dollar idea, at some point (or more likely at many points) you will have to explain it to someone. You will have to be clear and concise. They will need to understand what you or your product does. You might need to mention the target market and/or the target industry. Your pitch needs to include how you make money, if it is not explicitly clear for your product, service, or idea. Your pitch could include mention of competition and why you are different or better than they are.

The details of your elevator pitch will depend on your product, service, and situation. But it should focus on what the listener needs to know, how it benefits them, what you want them to know, and what your goal is for giving the pitch.

Think through these things and decide what elements need to be in your pitch. Then craft your elevator pitch (and perhaps have a couple of different versions ready, depending on who you might meet or for different end goals) and rehearse it. You need to be able to deliver it at any time on a moment's notice.

One of the most important meetings in my life lasted only sixty seconds. But prior to the meeting, I spent plenty of time thinking about what should be in my elevator pitch. Because of that I was one hundred percent ready. I had rehearsed the lines repeatedly. So, when the time came, I delivered the pitch to someone who was literally walking out the door while I was rushing across the room to meet them. Because of my preparation, I delivered it perfectly.

Before you go out in public and try to sell your product or, before that, if you go out to get support for your million-dollar idea (when you need money, people, resources, etc.), you need to identify what should be in the elevator pitch. Then you need to rehearse it until you know it cold, so you can deliver it at any time. You need to spend time constructing and rehearsing your lines until you can deliver them flawlessly.

The Results

Despite several marketing attempts not panning out as hoped, we still had a few "here and there" rentals. So our marketing efforts did have some impact, no matter how small.

However, as happens, the Universe still knew of my quest for a million dollars. It was still working to deliver it to me. Meanwhile, the flawless delivery of my elevator pitch led to the unexpected (but prepared for) event of becoming the official audio tour of the Top of the Rock Observation Center at 30 Rockefeller Plaza. This changed the focus of my business.

Rockefeller Center

I joined "NYC and Company," the city-run tourist-and-convention organization, for the cost of $900. I was officially part of the NYC tourist scene.

A month later, the man who ran the official NYC Visitor's Center called me. "They are re-opening the observation deck on the top of 30 Rock at Rockefeller Center. We are going for a behind-the-scenes visit—you should come with us. Do you want to visit 'Top of the Rock'?" he asked. "Of course! I'll test one of my devices up there," I answered.

The next afternoon, I went to NYC and Company's office on 7th Avenue to meet their contingent of people headed to Top of the Rock. The observation deck was part of the original buildings of Rockefeller Center but eventually closed. On September 11, 2001, the observation deck at the World Trade Center was destroyed. In 2006, the Top of the Rock Observation Deck re-opened, in part to fill that void.

I met the group. We walked through midtown Manhattan and found the operators of the observation deck. The deck was still under construction as part of its renovation. Regardless, we took the fancy express elevator to the deck and received a VIP tour.

However interesting the tour was, and however amazing the view was, I was there for one main reason: to find out if my GPS tour guide program would work on top of "30 Rock." Do GPS signals work on top of a building? Would the electronic equipment on top of the building interfere with the signals? Were the GPS signals accurate enough to do what I hoped would be possible?

The express elevators empty passengers into a beautiful sunlit enclosed glass room. We ventured outside to the main observation deck. I quickly reached into my briefcase to extract my GPS tour guide device. I quietly and secretively turned it on.

While our tour guide told us about the 360-degree views, I kept looking down at my device to see if it was catching a GPS signal. To calculate a location requires contact with four GPS satellites. I watched the counter to see how many satellites the device had contacted. It found two satellites immediately, then weakly, a third.

Our guide talked about the grand view of Central Park and the Hudson River. I was excited and nervous. I looked down, and there it was! Connection with four satellites—and a reading of a latitude and a longitude for a location! This meant the device acquired a signal. That was the first good news.

I flipped the device to a map program to see what the GPS signals were giving as our location. The map showed we were right on 30 Rockefeller Plaza. That was the second piece of good news!

Next, I needed to know if the GPS readings were accurate and if they would change in the right direction as the user walked around the observation deck. I walked with the group in one direction and the GPS readings changed in the correct direction and in roughly the correct increments.

I also needed to know if the readings would do the same thing in the other direction on a different part of the observation deck. Our tour group was looking south down the Hudson River, but I needed to be over on the other side of the building. I decided to make a run for it—and took off in the other direction, separating from the group.

The GPS signals worked flawlessly—since there is absolutely no interference between you and the satellites delivering the signals from miles above you. (The signals work less well in the concrete jungle canyons of Manhattan, since the tall buildings interfere with the signals and direct views of the satellites.) The signal was strong, and the coordinates seemed accurate. It looked like I was "in business."

Then I glanced up and saw an amazing sight. The view to the south from the observation deck was spectacular. On display was the entire southern part of Manhattan; the skyline dominated by the Empire State Building. You have likely seen a photo of the Empire State Building taken from this exact spot.

So, the view was spectacular. In addition, due to the ongoing construction, there was no barrier wall of any type between me and the edge of the roof. This added to the enjoyment of the view and the danger of the situation. I could get as close to the edge as I dared—and had a more and more amazing view with every step I took towards the edge.

I stepped slowly and carefully towards the edge of the building. An occasional taxi horn honked and echoed through the canyons of some of the most famous buildings in the world. Somewhere a jackhammer was creating progress and noise in the City that Never Sleeps. Finally, I was close enough to the edge of the building that the wind changed—I could feel the wind blowing up the side of the building. That was as close to the edge as I wanted to be.

I took one last look out at one of the most amazing views of my life—and retreated from the edge of the structure. I needed to find our tour group.

When I rejoined them, the man who ran the NYC Visitor's Center asked me the important question, "Does it work?" "Yes, it works great!" I informed him.

The Next Step

A few weeks later, I was back at Rockefeller Center, meeting with the men who run the operation. They wanted to know if my GPS tour guide would work at their observation deck and if I could create a special "Top of the Rock" version for them. They wanted an audio guide for their visitors.

Since I had already tested the device during our tour, I knew the device would work. "Yes, it will definitely work," I told them.

I left the office without any commitment from them, but I felt fairly confident I would be asked to supply and run the audio tour operation at the Top of the Rock Observation Deck. This was great news and to me, an honor.

Bad News

It took one month to receive an update from the folks at the Top of the Rock. The news they had for me was not good. They decided to do a deal with Microsoft. That company had a new device they wanted to launch and promote at the world-famous observation deck. Good publicity for them, bad business news for me.

That business was lost. Or so I thought.

A few days later, I happened to be talking with the man who programmed my GPS tour guide device. I told him what had happened at Top of the Rock and that they were going to go with a new Microsoft device. "That thing? It will never work," he said.

My programmer was one of the best in Silicon Valley. He had connections at Microsoft. He knew the guys working on the new product. They had told him candidly that it did not work and would never work.

For some reason I found myself again talking to the folks at Top of the Rock. I told them quietly, "Oh by the way, the Microsoft device is not going to work." These men were all New Yorkers and had no idea about my Silicon Valley connections. Who was I, the operator of a very small audio-guide business, to say that something from the gigantic Microsoft Company was not going to work?

However, it did not matter, as they had already struck a deal with Microsoft. It was "Game Over" for me as far as they were concerned. I went home and mostly forgot about them—I had other things on which to work.

The Phone Rings

Several months later, my phone rang. It was the manager of Top of the Rock. "Are you still interested in supplying us with an audio tour for Top of the Rock?" he asked. "Sure!" I answered. Two days later, I was once again in his office. He did not mention Microsoft, but I knew what had happened. I also knew he was in a bind and needed an audio tour device for his tourist attraction. I knew the business was mine.

"Are you *sure* it will work?" he asked one more time. I assured him it would work and tried not to laugh. The promised device from Microsoft had not worked, and now he was asking me if my device would work? For some reason it was amusing to me. I had no doubt it would work. I also knew he probably did not have any other options.

After this meeting, the high-priced lawyers from the real estate company that owns Rockefeller Center wrote a contract between them and my company. The terms were kind to me, as they wanted an audio tour more than they cared about money from the operation. I signed the contract and went to work on the special "Top of the Rock" version of my GPS tour guide.

Get to Work

The work included deciding what should be the points-of-interest for the audio guide, writing a script, collecting appropriate photos and videos, and recording the audio files—in five different languages. Of course, before you can record in five languages you must translate the script into five languages.

One of the highlights of the project was collecting appropriate photos. Rockefeller Center has an official archive office. In that office I met a wonderful woman who runs the archives. I explained to her what I was doing and why "corporate" had sent me to her. "Oh, you want the photo book," she said.

Then she took out an old black binder. She opened the book, and I saw the original contact sheets for *all* of the photos that were taken by a photographer one day during the construction of Rockefeller Center. Among the day's photographs was the original of one of the world's most famous photos—the construction workers sitting on a metal beam, eating lunch while high above the skyline of New York City.

The "Lunchtime" photo is famous all over the world. It has sparked countless parodies and tributes. Here I was, looking at the original contact sheet—the first print ever made of the photograph.

Two days later, I received digital copies of the photos I requested from the archives. The collection of material for the special "Top of the Rock" GPS tour guide was under way.

While compiling the material and putting together the system (e.g., collecting latitude and longitude coordinates for all the points-of-interest spots on the observation deck, then testing and re-adjusting them to make them work correctly), I met with the manager of the observation deck. We worked out the logistics of exactly where and how we would rent the devices. We decided a rental desk located underneath a gigantic chandelier would work. It placed us just after the ticket booth, a logical place to have the rental booth—or so I thought at first. The manager also agreed that Top of the Rock would build us a rental booth so it would match their interior.

While they built the booth, I finished putting together their system and hired ten people to staff the rental booth. I knew NYC had many actors who needed part time jobs, so I posted a small paid ad in the acting section of the Craigslist website. This proved to be a good thing to do, as I did not have any problems with the actors I hired. I did have a few problems with employees I hired from other sources.

Dress Rehearsal

After testing the system at the top of 30 Rock countless times by myself, it was time to have a "dress rehearsal." I contacted a select group of friends and contacts. I offered them free entrance to the observation deck and the chance to be the first people in the world to try the new "Top of the Rock" GPS audio tour. I had no problem obtaining volunteers.

Three days later, I had a small group of fifteen people gathered around me underneath the gigantic chandelier at the street level entrance of 30 Rockefeller Center. As I started to explain how to operate the device, I was instantly glad I decided to have this dress rehearsal. As I explained how to use the device, I realized it was stupid to do so. An audio device could explain by itself how it should be used. The only thing the user needed to know was how to play the first audio file—which would give instructions on how to use the device. That would free up my employees from the tedious task of delivering the instructions to every renter.

That night, I contacted my sound engineer. We recorded a new audio file. Then, I had to update all of the devices with the new audio file and updated computer information. After that, the final version of the tour was ready to go.

Curtain Up

I personally trained each of my employees on how to sell the device and show the guests how to use it. (That was now easier since all they had to do was press play on the first audio file and the device explained everything else to them.)

On our first day of operation, which required two shifts, I operated the rental desk alongside one of my employees. We took turns serving customers. I made it clear to my employees that I was not grading or judging them—I just wanted to figure out the best way to run the operation. Once I decided the employee could handle the work without me, I wandered around and watched the operation, trying to see how everything worked. After a while, I went home to relax—so I could return fresh for the second shift of the day.

The first few days of operation were all similar. I conducted many of the rental transactions myself, taking turns with my employees. I looked forward to the day when I would not have to be on-site and the rental operation could run without me.

Location, Location, Location—A Problem

It soon became apparent that we had a problem. Our sales numbers were lower than they should have been. My wandering around and watching the operation uncovered a source of the problem: We were only receiving half of the foot traffic we should have received.

The observation deck had a great ticket desk—and we were located right next to the ticket desk. Everyone who bought a ticket from the desk had to walk right by our rental booth (which had national flags on it representing each of the languages for which we had a tour). This seemed like a good location.

However, half of the visitors to the observation deck already had tickets! They bought tickets online or elsewhere. People with tickets did not come down to the ticket desk; they went in a different direction—which bypassed our rental desk. This meant we lost half of our foot traffic—which meant our sales were half of what they should have been.

There was another smaller problem with the location: It was right next to a small elevator that took guests up one floor to where their tour started. However, the guests thought this was the main elevator that they would take to the top. It was a logical thought, but the repercussions for us were that if the person saw our rental desk and saw the elevator arrive and open, they would forget about us and run to get on the elevator. This definitely cost us some sales—although nowhere near as many as losing the foot traffic did.

Everyone knows the old saying, "Location, Location, Location." I had heard it hundreds of times, but this experience showed me how true the maxim is. The physical location of your business can have a huge impact on your sales.

The Reviews

Our sales numbers were low, but we had wonderful feedback from the people who rented the GPS Audio Guide at Top of the Rock. Some people enjoyed the patriotic spin we had in one area. The audio featured quotes from John D. Rockefeller himself with ethereal "Up in the Sky" music provided by the St. Olaf College choir (my undergraduate college that has a phenomenal choir). I wrote the choir director a letter, and he provided exactly what was needed. Other people liked the catchy theme song, "We're Going Up!" which I wrote specially for the tour.

It is a gratifying experience to work hard on a project and receive thank-yous and other wonderful feedback from the intended audience. The customers enjoyed this special tour and that was important. The project also helped to pay the NYC rent of ten employees of the operation. I would have preferred our sales to be double or triple what we did, but I will always be proud of the work we did at Rockefeller Center.

Overview

I write this story of my experience at Rockefeller Center because it has a few important lessons:

- Be Prepared:

  The marketing material developed for the NYC GPS tour guide was very helpful in building some credibility with the people at Top of the Rock. The tour of Manhattan was ready, and I demonstrated the device to the management of the observation deck. We were prepared. When they called, I was ready to visit the next day.

- Hard Work Pays Off:

  All of the work done to date paid off when we went to obtain the contract for this special tour. It took a lot of work to develop the plan, the device, the software, the content, etc. However, when the observation deck at the Top of the Rock needed an audio tour, they had limited choices. I was one of them because of the work I had done to date. Because I had gone to the tourism convention, because I went to the hotel association meeting, and because I joined the NYC tourism group, I was introduced to the management of the observation deck. When Microsoft said they would not be supplying the tour, I was a local provider who could easily solve the problem. It took a lot of work, but it paid off.

- Don't Give Up:

  You never know exactly how things are going to turn out. For this opportunity, we were initially shut out when Microsoft said they would produce the tour. However, I left the door open to working with Top of the Rock and did not "burn any bridges." When Microsoft burned them, I was ready to help.

- Some Payoff Is Not Monetary:

  For the rest of my life, I know my work let tens of thousands of people listen to and enjoy the world's best audio tour. This by itself is worth something beyond money. I know I helped people pay their rent, which is sometimes very difficult to do in New York City. That is also worth something.

It is not possible to "monetize" my initial experience of being on the edge of the roof of 30 Rock, but it was certainly an experience I treasure. Later, because I received a special "all access" pass to the Rockefeller Center complex, I was able to enjoy the view from the observation deck many times. I was also able to walk to the base of the Christmas Tree the night of the famed "lighting of the Christmas Tree at Rockefeller Center." All of these things are valuable to me. They would not have happened had I not decided to have a million dollars.

Take a moment and think about the good things that will happen to you if you choose to follow the path provided in this book and by the story of my experience at Rockefeller Center. What good experiences will come to you? What new opportunities will you find?

How to Obtain Free Publicity

I f nobody knows about your business, plan, service, event, or idea, then it is much more difficult to obtain your million dollars. This chapter will help you acquire as much publicity as possible for your needs.

The secret to obtaining press coverage is that the media will help you—if you give them a good enough story. They *need* material. A daily newspaper needs to fill their pages every day. A daily television show needs to fill their programming on a daily basis. A daily radio show needs new material every day! So, to get coverage in the media you need to give them material they can use.

To help you acquire publicity it helps to have a **press kit** and a **press release**.

Your press kit is a collection of some of your marketing materials. You put everything into a nice folder and give it or send it to people who might help you promote your business. More on obtaining publicity later—but at this point realize that you want to make your business look as professional as possible. That is why you need a press kit.

If you call up a radio station and say, "help me promote my business," there is a small chance you will be successful. If you call them up, say that and then add, "I can send you our press kit," they will at least look at it—*and* you will have a much better chance of getting some coverage. Just the fact that you have a press kit puts you *much* further along the path of getting people's attention. Then, they are much more likely to realize you have a good and/or interesting business and they would be smart to cover it.

What Goes in Your Press Kit?

Your press kit can be as simple as a nice folder—which should be in the color scheme of your business—with a logo stuck to its cover. Sticking on a logo is as simple as running to an office supply store and buying some labels, such as Avery #8164. These are approximately 2.5-by-3.5-inch stickers. You use Microsoft Word or a similar program and download the template from the Avery website (avery.com). Some versions of Word actually have the templates already embedded in the software.

Put your logo and any additional information on each of the six sections of the document (you repeat the same thing six times, once for each label). I recommend you include your website and phone number on the label. Then use a color printer to print out the document on a sheet of the labels. Peel off one of the labels and stick it on the front of the folder. That is the outside of your press kit.

Here is what can go in it:

- Press release(s)
- Cover letter
- About the Owner page
- Sample of product(s)

- Business card
- Overview of your business
- Photos from your store and/or product
- A link to where they can download the photos online
- How-to-purchase sheet
- Copies of any press you have already received
- Copies of any marketing material you have created
- Customer reviews and/or thank-you letters from customers
- Anything else you think they might be interested in

You do not have to include everything listed above. You can also put in or not put in certain items based on cost or whether you think the recipient needs the item.

"Fancy" press kits developed by major ad agencies often show up in magazine editor's mailboxes. These kits are often contained in expensive special packaging. That is fine for a billion-dollar company. You do not need it.

If your material is good, the media will investigate your product and business. Your business and what it is about should then sell itself. An intriguing positioning and description are what will reel them in. It is your product or service's benefits and unique selling proposition (USP) that "sell" it. You do not need expensive packaging. The fact that you put together a coordinated, good-looking press kit is enough to garner some media attention.

Your Press Release

Your press kit should have at least one current press release in it. You can also include copies of any past releases.

You can pay a publicity agency a lot of money to develop a press release for you—or you can simply follow the example given here. It is an exact copy of the press release sent out to announce the unveiling of the world's first handheld GPS tour guide system. Everything between the date (13 September 2005) and the "#####," including those items, is part of the press release:

13 September 2005

For Immediate Release

High Tech Tour Guide Company Announces Handheld GPS Tour Guide System for New York City – New York, New York (September 13, 2005)

GPS Multi-Media Inc., a Manhattan-based technology and entertainment company announced this week that they have released "CityShow"—a handheld, GPS-based Tour Guide System for New York City. CityShow is now available to the public by rental from their website (www.cityshownyc.com).

CityShow, the "World's Coolest GPS Tour Guide System" is a revolutionary product that does not exist anywhere else in the world. Consisting of a handheld PDA computer, a GPS receiver, and a pair of headphones, CityShow delivers location-based tourist information to New York City visitors.

CityShow is extremely entertaining and helpful. As people wander the streets of Manhattan, CityShow tells them where they are, what they are near, and delivers appropriate history, stories, music, photos, and other information. The system even provides the locations of the nearest subway stations and public restrooms.

"It's definitely the coolest tour I have ever been on," says Matt Crawford of Houston, Texas. "It's amazing. It allows me to visit the city at my own pace, and the 'show' aspect of it was cool. It's not boring like a museum tour—it's really cool."

CityShow is available for rental in New York City by visiting: www.cityshownyc.com.

For further information visit the website or email press@
cityshownyc.com.

Full-sized digital photos (suitable for print) available upon
request.

About GPS Multi-Media Inc.:

GPS Multi-Media Inc. (www.cityshownyc.com & www.
gpsmm.com) is an entertainment and technology company
that specializes in location-based media and services.
Headquartered in New York, they offer the "CityShow" product
and derivations of it for the tourism, travel, and corporate
industries. Information about their main product is at www.
cityshownyc.com.

For Immediate Release Contact:

Brian Teasley
bteasley@gpsmm.com
646.414.1100
© 2005 GPS Multi-Media Inc.
#####

All of the preceding information will fit on a standard 8.5-by-
11 piece of paper. The "#####" is the symbol that notifies the
recipient of the release that they have received all of the content.

Notice that for the most part the press release sticks only
to the "facts" of the news. It does not embellish or try to
"sell" the GPS tour guide. You tell them *who* is making the
announcement, *what* the news is about, *when* it is, and *where*
it will be. If possible, you also work in your description of the
business or product and its positioning. Your press release gives
the journalists the famous "who, what, when, and where" that
makes up a good news piece.

You can embellish a bit—and the quote in the middle from
someone who tried the system (my sound engineer!) does that.

But if you talk about how fantastic the product, business, or service is, your press release ends up reading too much like a sales pitch. Recipients will ignore it.

To create your press release, simply amend the example so it fits your product or service. You can and should create releases for any newsworthy events. Obviously, you want to announce the release of your product or opening of your business. You could also send out a release for new products, special events, special sales, etc.

If you need more examples, suggestions, or tips, check out the resources section of: http://www.prweb.com/

That website has great information about how to write a press release. They have suggestions on what to do and what not to do. In general, the example provided here gives you a good idea of what you need.

How to Receive Press Coverage

Once you have a press release, a logo, and some other marketing materials (e.g., at least an "About the Owner" page, a list of benefits page, and a how to order page) you have enough material to create and fill a small press kit.

So how do you get press coverage? There are a few possibilities:

- You can hire a public relations (PR) agency to do the foot and phone work for you.
- You can send out your press release through a wire service.
- You can mail your press kit directly to contacts at media outlets.
- You can have members of the press hear about your business and contact you for information.
- You can run into them on the street and personally ask them to cover your business. I have run into a famous columnist in New York City on more than one occasion.

Always, always, *always* have a card regarding your product or service with you *at all times*. Better yet, have examples of your product with you (if feasible). You never know whom you might run into. It can and will happen anywhere at any time. If you are prepared, then you will be able to take advantage of the opportunity.

Let us look at some of the "how to get press coverage" options.

PR Agency?

Due to the cost, you probably do not want to hire a PR agency.

The people who work at a good public relations company are well connected. In part, you are paying for their "rolodex" of phone numbers.

They know the right contact names at all major media outlets (TV, radio, newspapers, magazines, etc.), and with a phone call or two they *might* be able to get coverage of your business. They are also usually *very* expensive. Again, due to the cost, you probably do not want to hire a PR agency, at least during your startup phase.

One company hired a PR firm to garner some publicity. The company paid the PR firm $15,000 per month as a "retainer." The company was not ready to use the PR firm, so the PR firm just kept billing $15,000 per month and collected the money. The PR firm *did not do anything* to earn the money!

My point is that a PR firm will be happy to take your money. They will also not promise you any results, because they cannot guarantee any results. So, it is better to spend your money, time, and efforts on other outlets.

On the other hand, if you have a friend in the PR business, ask them to help you. They have access to contacts, etc. and might be able to assist you at no cost.

This is another reason you need to have your press release and press kit ready to go *first*. If you tell your friend, "Hey, I have a press kit and a press release ready to go. Any chance you can help me get it in front of a few people?" they will be impressed that you have your act together. You have also made the process a lot easier, and it has a lot higher chance of being successful.

However, if you ask your PR friend to help you when you do not have a release ready to go and do not have a press kit ready to go, you are asking them to do that work for you. They will not want to do that and are much less likely to help you.

Using a PR Wire Service

You can send out a press release over a wire by yourself. The two easiest choices are www.prweb.com and www.prnewswire.com. PRWeb might be better for a pure online business, as it focuses on raising your search engine rankings and getting your story out via online sources. PR Newswire reaches the more "traditional" media sources, including newspapers and magazines across the country and the world. Another service, at www.pr-inside.com, is still a free service.

Originally, PRWeb was a free service. You submitted your release and it went out to a list of people who had opted-in to receive the press releases via email. The people who requested the emails *did* include writers at major news organizations. Over time, more and more people found out about the free service, so the quantity of the press releases submitted increased and the quality and value of the topics decreased.

To combat this, PRWeb instituted fees for the service. That is why you now must pay for distribution of your release. PR Newswire has a higher cost, but this reduces the release of "frivolous" news announcements. If it costs $1,000 to send out your release, you are going to make sure it is a newsworthy event before you publicize it.

It is unfortunate that the services are expensive for small businesses, but the cost weeds out many worthless press releases. Fewer worthless press releases increases the likelihood that your release will be received and read.

Key Words

When you send out your release, you need to know that some people will have set filters on their "receiving" capability. They want to receive news about certain topics. If your product or service involves one of their topics, then they actually *want* to receive your press release.

This means that you should insert as many appropriate key words into your press release as you can. That way you reach as many people who are looking for your news as possible.

If you use a PR newswire of some sort, *think about appropriate key words* and work them into your press release. Google's "AdWords" program has a key word tool that might help you select some additional key words.

You submit your news to the PR wire service and indicate which categories of news your release fits into. For example, "Arts and Entertainment" is a likely category if your product relates to art, music, or books.

If your product or service is relevant to a certain geographical area, that is actually good news in terms of PR distribution services. You select certain geographies for distribution, and some people may have signed up to receive *only* the press releases that relate to that geography. That actually *increases* your chance of coverage.

Sending Out Your Press Kit to the Press

You definitely will want to send out your press kit to anyone you think should cover your story. Certainly you will send it to the following people and organizations:

- Heads of the appropriate sections of all of your local (or national) newspapers
- Programs that cover your topic on any local radio stations—note that you probably need to specify the name of the program and the host to increase the chances of your kit reaching them.
- Magazines in your industry (Possibly with a tailored article for them to print. Be sure to let them know you can provide it electronically so they can cut and paste the material easily.)
- Websites related to your product or service
- Podcast and blog operators related to your product or service
- Heads of any organizations related to your product or service. This may be a local or national endeavor. It depends on your topic.
- Anyone else who might be interested that you can think of

Include a cover letter and tailor it to each recipient.

Many people would never think to try to market their business or product via a major local radio station. However, I think it is a great idea. Why? Because program directors are looking for interesting programming, and they have already covered national stories. A local "up-and-coming" businessman with a unique topic might be very interesting to them.

If you storm in with a truly new, fresh news story with good product or service, the radio program directors (and other media people) might just give you a shot. "You mean you have a product with current, edgy insights related to my show's audience? Let's hear it!" will be their response. Radio stations love breaking interesting stories. It helps with their "cool" factor. They might even end up holding an event at your location or something like that. Not such a bad result from sending out a press kit!

A cover letter to such a radio show should include something along the lines of, "Hey, I know you don't usually cover products for sale online from local businessmen in your 'New Local Business News' program, but I have a brand-new product that is going to blow people away. I think your listeners might love it. If you have a chance, please give it a once over. You can find out more information at: yourwebsite.com."

The included press release would mention the business owner is available for interviews, etc. Make sure they know you can be available at a moment's notice, if that is possible. You never know when a guest cancellation might occur, and you will receive a frantic phone call. I have had everything from 15-minutes notice to 48-hours notice for radio interviews.

Don't think it could happen to you? I had a business with a news story that I thought would fit in well with a certain program on WOR radio in New York City. WOR is a powerhouse AM radio station based out of Manhattan. They are one of the original "clear channel" radio stations (as opposed to the corporation now known as "Clear Channel") which means you can hear their signal from a very far distance away, especially at night.

I put together a press kit in the exact manner described in this book. Two weeks later, I was sitting discussing my idea with the host of one of the station's shows. It was that simple. I put together a nice press kit with a couple of press clippings, a post card, and a couple of press release examples. I included a brief cover letter that listed two or three reasons why I thought their audience would like to hear about the story. I sent it to the program, care of the radio station. They emailed me and we set up a time to meet. It can happen to you, too.

Since you already have a press kit, it will not take longer than a few minutes to call a radio station or television station and ask them how to make a submission to a specific show. Alternatively, you can ask for their guidance as to appropriate shows, but then you are asking them to do work for you— and that is always a bad idea. Do you think the person who answers the phone really wants to help you that much? So do a little research, and you will be on the right track.

Who Else Do You Send it To?

Whom do you send your press kit to if you do not have a list of contact names? Call or email the publication and ask them. You might want to check their website first as they might have the contact information listed there.

For example: http://www.timeout.com/newyork/section/get-listed

Time Out is a weekly entertainment magazine in New York City (and other cities) that has a calendar of events. If your company is in NYC and having an event, they make it easy to tell you what to do to be listed on their calendar. Your local publications likely have similar listings of how and who to contact.

One or two lines in a magazine might not do much in terms of traffic to your event, but every little bit helps. Moreover, it is a combination of exposure to your product that drives people to buy it—so every little reminder you can have is good. If they list your event or you get a product mention in a publication, at the minimum you will be able to say, "as mentioned in (publication name here)" on your website.

When you call the publication or station, you simply call the main phone number and say something like, "Hello, I have a cool new product or service, and I'd love to send a press kit to the appropriate people at your publication/station. Can you tell me who that is or transfer me to somebody who would know?"

Call all your local publications, radio stations, and television stations and obtain the contact info. *Then* look through the publications and find the names of additional people you think would be interested in your information.

For radio stations, listen to their shows and/or visit websites to determine appropriate shows for your content. Send a press kit to them as well as the people on your collected contact list.

If you happen to live in a smaller area, or came from a smaller area, that might actually be a good thing. Local papers are looking for local news. If you creating a new product or service is a "local boy does good" type of story, then play it up, and make sure they know about your story.

Trust me, this is a difficult thing to pull off if you live in New York City and your local paper is the *New York Times*. However, using the methods in this book, I have received coverage in the *New York Times*.

Note:

Major monthly magazines have deadlines about two or three months before the date that appears on the cover. So, if you want your news covered in certain issues, you need to plan accordingly and get your news to them early.

Weekly publications usually need a week's advanced notice for listings.

Publications that will write a story based on your news need about two to three weeks advance notice (maybe more, maybe less) to cover your story. Make sure you give them plenty of advance notice or they will not be able to cover your news even if they want to.

Note: *Do not send out your press release for the release of your product or service until you are ready to sell it.* If you are not ready to sell your product, do *not* waste the publicity. Wait until you are ready to go! Said another way, get your act together early. Figure out how you are going to sell your product or service and get that set up first.

If you have things set up early, you will be able to take advantage of all of your publicity and sell as much product as possible. Do not be like the Kodak Corporation.

Ready, Set... Wait?

At some point in the late 1990s there was a "revolution" in photography—something about being able to take panoramic photos. The digital photo revolution was just about to hit like a tidal wave, but Kodak and other camera manufacturers were pushing a new "panoramic" photo capability.

The marketing and PR departments did a great job of garnering publicity. There were stories in many publications and they even had a front-page story in the *Wall Street Journal*. Very, very good stuff.

Unfortunately, nobody had checked with the manufacturing and distribution portions of the company. When the publicity hit the streets, there were *no cameras* available for purchase. They were not in any stores, anywhere. It was *six months* until the cameras hit the retail shelves! Highly amusing, unless you sell Kodak cameras. In that case, it was a huge wasted opportunity.

When/How

Make sure you have enough advance notice for the publication when you send your kit to it. Make the editor's life easy—do not put them on a deadline, because they will not work to it. Instead, they will throw your stuff away.

Put your press kit folder inside a large envelope. If you have not printed your own envelopes at a print shop (there is no reason you need to), simply create a "return address label" and stick it on the center of the envelope. Use the Avery #8164 (you can download a template from their website). Put your logo and return address on the top half of the label. The bottom half is where you will write or type in their address. Stick the label in the center of the envelope, insert your press kit (do not forget to include a tailored cover letter), and send it to them!

Do not call them to see if they received it (except if you have an existing relationship with them or some other extraordinary situation). Follow up with a postcard a week or two later to remind them—if you have not heard anything. If you do receive coverage from them, a thank-you note is a good idea, especially if you can address it to a specific person.

Will You Get Publicity? (and How I Got Mentioned on "Regis!")

If you send out a press release, maybe will you receive coverage. Maybe not. But here is an important secret: media outlets *need* your news. Without news, they wither. *The better your story, the better your chances of getting coverage.*

As an entrepreneur, I have many different areas of work. A few years back I started a "Data and Analysis for Marketing" service for ad agencies and other marketing groups. I wanted to receive some publicity, so I thought about what special things I could come up with that might be "newsworthy."

Since the business was about data, I figured it should have something to do with that. After thinking for a few days, I decided to take the U.S. Census Data and use it to come up with a list of "Top 10 Cities in Which to Find a Single, Rich Man."

I did the analysis, set up a bunch of related files on my website (top 10 list, a list of the ranking of all U.S. cities, biographic information, information about my services, etc.), and sent out a press release via prweb.com.

I waited a couple of days... and nothing happened. The release had been read by quite a few people on the service (they track that information), but there did not seem to be any coverage. At the end of the third day, I was driving home through a scenic portion of Connecticut after speaking at a conference. I checked my voice mail. There was a message from a reporter at the *New York Daily News*. He wanted to ask me a couple of questions about my story.

The cell phone reception stunk (thanks, Sprint) so I could not get a connection to return the call until I returned to my office. By then, the folks at the *Daily News* had gone home. I figured I had missed my chance, at least immediately. I was wrong.

The next morning, I was preparing to leave on a trip to Boston. The phone rang. It was KSFO radio in San Francisco. "Hey, we're calling about your 'Top 10 Rich Man' story and we'd like to put you on the air in 15 minutes if we could," said the voice on the phone. "Ok, sure!" I answered. Fifteen minutes later, I was talking via AM radio to tens of thousands of people in the Bay Area of San Francisco. The hosts asked me about the methodology I used to create the list. They asked why I thought the Bay Area made the list. It was an enjoyable interview, and I am certain the hosts were happy with the segment.

We ended the segment and I hung up the phone. The phone rang again. It was a production assistant from the show *The View* on ABC television. "We wanted to confirm a few things in regard to your story," he said. "Ok!" I replied. The production assistant mentioned the article in the *Daily News*.

After the call, I figured I should see if I could find the article. I ran down to my nearest newsstand and bought a copy of the *Daily News*. I flipped through the pages trying to find the paragraph or two about my story. I could not find it.

Confused, I literally went back to the front page and said, "Ok, it's not on the front page." Then I turned the page to scan inside. "Ok, it's not on page two inside…" Page 3 had a picture of Gisele Bündchen wearing a snake, plus some other huge article. That certainly was not our couple of paragraphs. Then, my subconscious said something like "ahem!" to me. That is when I noticed my name on the page. It turned out that the *entire* page three of the *New York Daily News* (except for the photo of Gisele) was about my "Top 10 Places to Find a Rich Man"!

That was crazy.

I went back to my office. I wanted to track press mentions, mainly to be able to use them for my own marketing purposes, so I emailed some colleagues and said, "Hey, if you happen to see mentions of this, please let me know." A couple of hours later one of them emailed me back. "You might not believe this, but you were just on *Regis*," he said.

Apparently to fill time—the media has hours of airtime they need to fill every day—some shows read from newspapers and comment on the stories. Well, my "story" was prominently placed in a major New York newspaper, so Regis Philbin read and commented about my survey and me.

CNN Radio, stations in Texas, San Francisco, Wisconsin, Pittsburgh—and a couple of others I do not remember—interviewed me. An Associated Press writer wrote a story about the list and put it on the AP wire. One hundred newspapers across the country featured my list—and it was covered by numerous radio stations throughout the U.S.

My website traffic sharply increased. In a couple of days I probably had ten to twenty thousand visitors. I received a ton of press clippings. For about two weeks people I knew treated me very differently. Suddenly I was famous. I knew it was a "15 minute" type of thing, but it sure was strange. I even received a multiple-page letter in the mail from a woman complaining that her city should not be on the list because the men in her town were awful.

How much business did I receive from the publicity (this is a book about making a million dollars, in case you think I forgot)? None—at least not directly. I did send out a couple of proposals to people who contacted me from the story, but I did not make any money directly off the publicity. However, the press clippings definitely helped convince other prospects who came along later. Being in major news outlets does wonders for your credibility.

If I were to do the same thing today, I would do one thing different. I would have the full list of all U.S. cities and where they ranked available on my website but behind a PayPal button. You send me $4.99 or maybe $9.99 via PayPal, and you can then instantly download the list. It would be an easy way to make some spending money.

Your "Take Away" Points from This Story

This story has a few important points.

First, I had a unique idea. Admittedly it was a bit silly (I am embarrassed to say it made the front page of a Pittsburgh paper while a story about U.S. soldiers' deaths was on page four). Certainly "where to find single rich men," based on U.S. census data, is compelling to some people.

Second, I purposely released the story in February—and prior to Valentine's Day. January and February are traditionally slow news months. Something has to fill the airwaves and print space, so the media outlets need content. *Even Regis needs content* (he had the number one morning national television program for many years). So do not think your story will not be covered. If it is interesting to some people—and especially if it is "news"—then it can get coverage.

I thought somebody would cover my story with a Valentine's Day angle. But I struck out completely with that idea. Maybe I did not release it early enough—or maybe that was just not quite the right idea.

That is a very important piece of knowledge: many things you will do in your marketing will not work the way you planned. They might not work at all, in terms of directly selling your product or service. But some things you do will work. You will not know which ones will work until you try.

Get a Gimmick

Ken Davenport is the producer of a show in New York City called *My First Time*. He came up with a gimmick—anyone who is a virgin would be allowed into the premiere for free. He put the word out, and the Associated Press picked up the story. That means it is covered all over the country. He found a unique marketing angle and received a huge amount of publicity from the story.

So, what can you do that ties into your product or service and is a worthy story? Is there some unique angle you can think of? Maybe you can conduct a promotion with a local (or national) store, restaurant, etc. that might have something in common with your product or service? Does your product or service relate to a certain holiday (e.g., Valentine's Day, St. Patrick's Day)? Does your product or service relate to a time of year (winter snow shoveling, spring gardening, summer barbeques) or event? Spend some time thinking about these types of questions to help you produce your marketing and press release plan.

For example, the Puerto Rican Day parade is a huge event in New York. If you had a product or service from or about Puerto Rico, you might be able to obtain some coverage in conjunction with the parade. If you simply are Puerto Rican and open a business the week of the parade, you might earn coverage as someone who has "done good" in the community.

What upcoming events can you leverage for your product or service? Is there some event or date for which media might be looking for stories?

Remember that the newspaper, magazine, radio, etc., people all have airtime to fill. Give them something they can use. Have photos, videos, MP3s, etc. ready for them on your website. Make it as simple as possible for them to cover your story.

Publicity "Stunts"

Almost anything you can do to attract attention to your product or service is a good thing. The ability to think of and pull off a unique publicity stunt is something that requires a creative mind.

The "My First Time" press release announcing that virgins would be let in free to the show is a great "stunt." The "Top 10 Cities in Which to Find Single, Rich Men" story qualifies as a "stunt," too.

Bus and airline companies start new routes and announce that initial fares are $1. This receives press attention. Some Broadway shows sell tickets the first day for a dirt-cheap price, tying the price to the name of the show if possible.

Trying to obtain public attention, some companies have secretly paid fake customers to set up tents outside a company store so the company can say, "People are already in line, camping out, to buy this new product..."

Think about your target market and where they could be exposed to your story and business. Think about the "media" (or medium) that is involved or is best to get involved, whether it's print, radio, television, online, a street corner, or other location. What does that media need? What do they need a story about? What would they want to cover? Is there something you can do to create some "buzz" about your business—or even to create some kindhearted controversy? What would work well on the street and get attention? What would the local paper cover? Can you conduct an event they might cover? If they do not cover it, you can send them photos and a short story after the fact. You never know what they might cover. If it is fifteen minutes before deadline and they have one space in their newspaper to fill and you just sent them a cool photograph... in it goes.

Do Something Different

If you do something unique, you will be noticed. So, do something different. Something. Anything. Figure it out and do it.

If you simply mimic everybody else's advertising, everybody else's approaches, everybody else's messages, everybody else's products or services, then what are you telling your target audience? You are telling them you are just like everybody else! Why should they bother to purchase your product or service if it is no different from any other?

The reason you are selling your product or service, the reason you are advertising it, the reason you are putting it out there is (or at least should be) *because it is different* than other products/services. If it is not, then there is no reason for anybody to buy it. Your marketing needs to come from a position of "we have a unique offering" rather than from a "we need to sell product" perspective.

This applies to your press release and press kit efforts, but it also applies to your product or service and your marketing efforts overall. You can and need to come up with some unique ideas. It will greatly increase your chance of getting noticed and getting attention, both from the press and from individuals. That will help you *sell more of your product/service.*

Viral Marketing

One of the current buzzwords is "viral marketing." This refers to any piece of marketing (text, photo, video, graphic) you produce which is shared by multiple people. Each person with whom it is shared also shares it with multiple people. The effect is exponential growth in the number of people that see it, following the pattern of growth a virus takes when it infects people.

The term refers to online marketing, but it is the same pattern exhibited by the "Top 10 Cities to Find Single Rich Men" piece. It first appeared in one newspaper, then used by several television shows, then many newspapers, and then radio stations all across the country. It all started from the press release that I created on my computer.

One way to achieve or cause viral marketing is the same manner described in this chapter. Do something unique and interesting that produces a good story. Whether the piece should be an article, a video, a photo, or graphic depends on your story and how it is best conveyed. Do whatever you need to get the story to the right places. If the story is good, it will be shared.

An Alternative

An alternative method of acquiring viral marketing takes advantage of the same need for more content and news mentioned earlier. At the moment, there is an ecosystem for news that works like this:

- Small blogs start news.
- Well-known blogs take the "best" of this news and create a larger story and more exposure.
- Legacy media (newspapers, TV, radio) use the well-known blogs for stories and source them as "Such and such website is reporting."

The problem with this "reporting" is that it allows for stories which are not true to be broadcast on large television and radio stations. The large publications deflect blame by tagging the story with "So and so is reporting." So even if the story is not true, it is true that somebody is reporting it.

To use this ecosystem for your marketing, focus on a few appropriate smaller blogs that feed into a larger blog in which you are interested. There is a tool at buzzstream.com that will help you find appropriate blog sites. You send your press release or simply an "email from a reader" to these blogs. They need content, so they publish your story. With a little luck or a little controversy, a larger organization will pick up your story, and things can go viral from there.

It is also possible appropriate blogs will pick up your story simply from using a press release service. Some blogs use key word searches to find appropriate new press releases and automatically post the press release verbatim.

Doing Press Interviews

If/when you are asked to do an interview with the press, be smart about it. Practice ahead of time. Know what you want to say. Rehearse it.

You will want to have this prepared ahead of time and ready to go at a moment's notice, because you might receive a phone call from a radio station saying they'd like to put you on the air either immediately or within a few minutes. If you have a "talking points" sheet ready to go, that will be of great assistance to you.

What should you say? Well, you already know what your product or service is about—and you know your positioning statement (how does your product differ from the competition's). If you do not say those things during your interview, verbatim, then you failed. You might also want to include some version of your elevator pitch.

Also, if you have no experience doing interviews, consider getting some help. Find somebody who does have on-camera experience. Cameras, lights, etc., are all very distracting and they take some getting used to. You'll start wondering where you should put your hands, turn your head, turn your body... how should you sit... what should you wear.... All of this will distract you from delivering your marketing message.

I sat next to a friend of mine as she did an in-audience skit with David Letterman. I sat through the afternoon rehearsal (with a stand-in for Letterman) and then attended the taping of the show. Right before the segment, I was amazed how nervous *I was*—and I was not even going to be doing anything!

The fact that Letterman was about to come over, and the cameras were going to be on, really made me nervous. I am embarrassed to admit it, but I am also smart enough to know to have somebody with experience handle things they will be better at than I will. My friend, a professional actress, nailed the bit, and the show had a great segment because of it.

If you are personally going to do an important television appearance, start studying what goes on at other similar shows (and the one you will appear on) and learn what works and what does not. Copy the good things, and avoid the bad things. Practice ahead of time. Rehearse.

If by chance someone is going to do an interview or appearance for you, work with them to make sure you get your product or service description, positioning statement, and product or service selling information into their head. When the host says, "Tell us a little bit about the product or service," that is their cue for you to parrot your description and positioning.

Feed the Monster

The Internet and cable television have changed communication forever. Twenty-four-hour news channels need content to put on the air for the entire day. Websites need fresh content to keep viewers/visitors coming back for more. Radio stations need programming for twenty-four hours each day. Magazines and newspapers need new content every day.

The need for content plus the ability to communicate worldwide and quickly makes for great opportunities for entrepreneurs who want to get the word out about their new product or service. If you come up with a good story and prepare yourself correctly, you will obtain the publicity you seek. That will propel you one step closer to your million dollars.

Will They Steal Your Idea?

------◆------

It is a common worry among people with a potential money-making idea: how do I talk with people about my idea? What if they steal my idea? Do I need to have them sign a non-disclosure agreement (NDA) before I talk with them? Because you have read some of this book, you might understand why you do not need to be too worried about this happening to you and your million-dollar idea.

First, if you use the methods of this book you will realize the idea is yours. Not only should you feel it "belongs" to you, but it likely has something to do with you and your background. Because of that, you are best situated to make the million dollars from the idea. To be clear, the idea was given to you through some unknown power/energy source; it does not belong to you. However, you are its custodian—granted permission to have the idea and act upon it, especially because you likely have specialized knowledge that has something to do with the idea.

Secondly, simply having an idea is far from enough to make a million dollars. People discussed the idea of a handheld GPS tour guide before I had the idea for it. However, nobody acted upon the idea. Nobody actually made it happen. I was the first person in the world to create a handheld GPS tour guide for three reasons. First, I had some specialized knowledge related to the concept. Second, I was looking for a good idea. Third, I decided to pursue and work on the idea once it came to me. I took action. Nobody who had previously thought about a GPS tour guide did this.

Venture Capital and Execution

If you are going to a venture capital firm and asking them to invest in your business, you do not need to worry much about them stealing your idea. They make their money by investing and giving guidance to fledgling companies. They do not make money by starting new businesses—they make their money by helping new businesses get started.

By itself, having a million-dollar idea does not earn you a million dollars. Having a million-dollar idea and executing a plan to turn the idea into reality—that is how to earn a million dollars.

As a user on an online forum put it:

"You're not afraid of them stealing your idea. You are afraid of them out-executing you. The solution: stop f-ing around and get to work. If you are truly passionate about your idea, no one will be able to catch you.

"Proof: Would you be fearful of divulging every detail of your business idea to your neighbor's 10-year-old kid? No. You know there is zero chance the kid could out-execute you. It is not about the idea. It's about execution."

But Beware

There are some ideas that are exceptions to the general rule. If it is very easy to execute your idea, then if the wrong person hears about it, it is possible they will steal your idea. This is true for any idea that is simple to replicate. It is also likely someone will try to copy or steal your idea if you have a successful business, especially if it is easy to replicate.

If you think a specific person might be able to replicate your business, you should not talk with them about your idea or your business. If they can easily do what you are going to do or have done, what is to prevent them from taking away some of your customers and some of your business?

When the iPhone first came out, a handful of computer programmers made incredible amounts of money in days. The programmers created and released games for the device. Game playing on a phone was a complete novelty, so users were ready for even the simplest of games.

As word got out about how much money the programmers were making, others quit their day jobs at engineering companies. They realized they could make a year's salary in a week if they wrote a popular game. The success of the first games caused other programmers to try to replicate that achievement. Since Apple made it relatively easy for people to sell games (or any other application) to iPhone users, there was little to stop other programmers from joining the first developers.

So, if your idea or success is easy to replicate, you should proceed with caution, but understand it is very likely someone will steal or copy your successful idea at some point.

The Mud Truck

A man in New York City started a very successful "Street Coffee" business. He converted a Con Edison electric truck into a coffee-selling truck. He painted the truck bright orange, played rock music from it, hung an American flag on the side of it, and parked on a street right between three Starbucks locations. Within a week, the story of the Mud Truck was literally news around the world, with coverage reaching Tokyo and Sydney.

The coffee-truck business was successful—and the man expanded the business to three trucks. Seeing the success firsthand, one of the guys who worked selling coffee in the truck thought, "I can do this on my own." He decided to copy/steal the successful idea.

The employee quit, bought his own truck, and painted it bright orange. His truck looked just like one of the three Mud Trucks. Only the name on the side of the truck was different. The move was a blatant rip-off of the successful Mud Truck idea. The idea thief even hung up an American flag. The result? For better or worse, his rip-off creation was and still is a success.

So, if you blaze a trail and are successful, do not be surprised if someone steals your idea and replicates it. If you wish to avoid this, you will need to develop a franchise system or some other mechanism to dissuade people from executing your idea on their own. Can you make it profitable for someone else to join you in some way?

Unfortunately, there is no way to ensure someone will not try to steal your idea. However, patents and trademarks exist to help you with this problem.

Making the Complex Simple

You can boil down this book to the words "Come up with a million-dollar idea and make it happen." But the reality of making a million dollars is more complicated than the simplicity of that statement. If you read this book carefully and study it well, you will understand the components required for you to reach your million dollars. You will understand the "complexity"—and once you understand it will not be complex.

You will see and understand a process that many men have used to make millions of dollars. You will understand why many people never make a million dollars. You will understand more about people and about yourself. You will understand why you do not have to worry too much about someone stealing your million-dollar idea, unless it is very easy to replicate.

An idea by itself is not worth much. A good idea combined with everything else discussed in this book is valuable. When I made my million dollars, nobody had created a handheld GPS tour guide system. The technology was available, and people discussed the idea. But why had nobody created such a system?

If the idea by itself was worth a million dollars, other people should have had the million dollars, not me. But they did not execute on the idea. I did.

Here's to the Naysayers

D uring the course of your journey to your million dollars, people will tell you your idea will not work. There are many reasons why someone may tell you your idea will not work, but none of them are important. Ignore these people.

The only person's opinion to which you should listen is a subject matter expert you know and trust. Listen to this person and *decide on your own* if your idea will or will not work based on your plans. You may be doing something different that the expert has not thought about, or you may know something he does not know. You are the expert on your idea. Collect information from subject matter experts during your research, but only you can decide if your idea will or will not work.

The Man Who Did Not Get a Good Grade

In 1965, a business school student wrote a term paper describing the need for and a system for delivering time-sensitive packages. Industries including medicine, computers, and electronics had a need for quick delivery of medicines and parts. The existing method of using passenger airplanes did not deliver packages as quickly as the student thought was needed. A dedicated system could deliver packages more quickly and fill a business need.

His professor was not impressed and only gave the student a mediocre grade.

Six years later the student, Frederick Smith, bought controlling interest in an Arkansas-based aviation company. He changed the name of his company to "Federal Express" and in two years his company made its first profit. Today the company is worth over $46 billion. So, you see, a business school professor might not be an expert on business ideas.

Remember this when someone says your idea will not work! The idea could be worth over a billion dollars, and a business school professor might say it is only an average idea.

A Star is Coming

After graduating from the superb Northwestern Drama School in Chicago, actor/comedian Billy Eichner moved back to NYC. In the early 2000s, he was a complete "unknown" in the city of millions. Some of his first NYC shows were in a place called "The Tank." The black box room did not even have a stage, just a few chairs for the audience members and higher chairs for the actors in the show. At one show, there were eight people in the audience.

Small audiences did not dissuade Billy Eichner from continuing with his plan and desire. He persisted. He continued with his small shows, slowly gaining some traction in terms of a following. His persistence paid off. His audience size grew from eight to twenty to fifty, eventually filling a 99-seat theater.

Meanwhile, he knew someone who owned a restaurant—and gave a series of shows in the basement of it. One evening a former cast member of *Saturday Night Live* had dinner in the restaurant. She decided to check out the comedy show in the basement. After five minutes, she was intrigued enough to watch the entire show. After the show, she met Mr. Eichner. Based on a phone call from the SNL alumni, the next Sunday a large article about Billy Eichner appeared on the front page of the Art and Entertainment section of the *New York Times*.

The following Saturday night, after a week fielding phone calls from potential agents, Billy Eichner opened his show with the perfect line: "I have never given away so many free tickets to rich white men before in my life!" With that, he was further on his way to success. His own television show followed, and in 2019, he signed with Universal Pictures to write and star in a romantic comedy movie.

His story shows the reason one needs to persist. In fifteen years, because of his persistence, he went from audiences of eight people to the big screen where millions of people will see him. His bank account has grown proportionally, too. If he had given up because of small audiences or for any other of a number of possible reasons, he would not have reached the success level of writing and starring in a major motion picture.

The conclusion of this story: Do not let anyone persuade you that your good idea might not work. Do not let anyone tell you it is not possible.

My Story

As part of my development of the world's first handheld GPS tour guide system I became an expert on GPS signals in New York City. I knew where they worked perfectly. I knew where they were the most inaccurate. I knew they could be affected by thick clouds in the sky and surrounding tall buildings.

I also knew from research and information from other entrepreneurs that I might encounter people who would tell me my idea would not work. It was still a surprise to me when it happened. Moreover, it happened not once, but on several occasions!

I was at an NYC tourist/convention meeting of some sort, and people asked what I did. I explained that I had the world's first handheld GPS tour guide. One man said, "That will never work," and began to tell me why it would not work. I listened carefully at first. My scientific training taught me to always listen to opposing ideas, as you never know when they might be right.

But in this case, the man was wrong. For example, he talked about cars receiving the wrong directions from their GPS-based voice guidance systems. My system was not going to give driving directions. In addition, in this case, I was by far more of an expert on the topic than he was. In fact, he did not know anything about how GPS signals worked or how my tour guide system worked. But that did not prevent him from having and voicing his contrary opinion.

Why did he do this? I do not have any idea. But there he was, telling me why my idea would not work. This surprising phenomenon happened more than once. For seemingly no reason someone felt compelled to tell me why my idea would not work. What is it that makes people do this? We will leave the answer for psychologists to debate.

Perhaps if I was weak in the mind or thought their opinions had fact-based merit, I would have let their comments influence me. But I persisted with my plans. I had a good idea, I had a good plan, and I had a strong desire to make the plan happen. I was going to make the world's first handheld GPS tour guide. I also knew it would work, especially after I conducted my initial research.

Join the Club

The path to your million dollars has twists and turns in it. Along the way, you may encounter temporary setbacks and problems with which you must deal. You may also have people who know nothing about your idea tell you it will not work. Ignore them.

Your desire, faith, and idea given to you by the Universe will propel you towards what you request. Someone telling you why it will not work should be no match for you and your idea.

Here are some things to consider to push you along the path to your million dollars:

- Multiple publishers rejected the manuscript for the first Harry Potter novel before one accepted it. They only accepted it because the editor did not want to read the sample chapter, so he gave it to his eight-year-old daughter. She insisted upon knowing what happened next, so the publishing house bought the script for their standard minimum. The initial print run was 500 copies, indicating they did not expect to sell many of the books. The author is now a billionaire.
- One publisher told Nabokov that his book *Lolita* was nauseating and should be buried. The top publishers in New York City all rejected the book. But Nabokov persisted, publishing the book in Paris with Olympia Press. The first 5,000 copies sold quickly, so the

publishers that had rejected the book changed their minds. Today, it has sold over 50,000,000 copies.

- Hemingway, John Le Carré, George Orwell, and the Beatles were all rejected when they were first starting. They all persisted and ended up selling millions and millions of their products. It happens the same way with other business ideas.

So, when someone makes the mistake of telling you why your idea will not work or rejects you in some form, you are in good company! Some of the richest people in the history of the world were all rejected.

But these people persisted. They had the required elements, discussed in this book, to make their mark on the world. They knew what they had to do to make their millions of dollars. They continued along their path until the Universe delivered to them the money/energy they requested.

Disney RideCard

Twenty years before I created the world's first handheld GPS tour guide system, I had an even better multi-million-dollar idea. However, I left the millions of dollars sitting on the table. They were mine for the taking, but I left them there. Why? Because I simply did not follow through with what I needed to do to get the money. That happened because I did not know what I needed to do. Read this, and do not let it happen to you.

You may know of Disneyland amusement park's "FastPass" system. It is their computerized system that allows you to make a reservation at your favorite ride and not have to wait in line. The system was my idea.

I was the first person in the world to conceptualize and propose using computers to create a ride reservation system for use at amusement parks. It was a great idea. Guests at a park would not have to stand in long lines. They would be free to enjoy the park and buy more concessions and souvenirs.

I did some things, but unfortunately not enough things, to make it happen. In simple language: I screwed up. In more complicated language: I did not do everything necessary to complete the process—to change my idea (a thought in my head) into its final real-world equivalent: millions of dollars in my pocket.

This book exists to help you understand and complete the process.

How it Happened

In 1989, I had an Apple 2e computer system. I taught myself basic programming and wrote programs for money. One day I was at the Great America amusement park north of Chicago. I was standing in a 45-minute line waiting to go on the flume ride. It was fun to ride the plastic logs on the water, but it was not fun at all to wait for 45 minutes.

"Somebody should do something about this," I said to my friend, "Standing in line is stupid." At that moment, the idea for the system flashed into my head. It was a simple and obvious application of existing technology. Simply have a computer at each ride record each guest's identification number. Calculate the wait time and tell them what time to return.

I was 25 and knew nothing about business. However, I did know the system would work. I put together a very short presentation about it. After that, I had no idea what to do next.

I managed to find the phone numbers of about fifteen major amusement parks in the United States, including Disneyland in Anaheim, California. I started making phone calls. I called and said to whoever answered the phone something like, "Hi, my name is Brian Teasley, and I have an idea for a ride reservation system. You know, so your guests do not have to stand in the long lines? Who should I talk to about this?"

It was a blunt, straightforward approach. And guess what? It worked! I talked to several important "decision making" people.

They were generally vice-presidents of operations for the park. Some said they were not interested (or did not know what I was talking about, since computer systems were not ubiquitous at the time), but a few were interested, and we talked more.

One day I was having lunch at my parent's house where I was living for the summer after finishing graduate school. The phone rang. My mother answered it and whispered to me, "Brian, it's for you. It's Disneyland."

So, I talked with the head of "Tomorrowland" at Disneyland. He must have been confused, calling someone and having their mother answer the phone. We had a good discussion, but he decided to pass on the idea and sent me a nice letter in the mail saying "thanks, but no thanks—not at this time." I still have the letter. It took ten years until Disney finally debuted their FastPass line reservation system.

The Wrong Attitude

I was 25 years old at the time. I thought I was not as important as the "important" men I talked with on the telephone. I thought they knew better than I did. I was wrong. I was as important as they were. In fact, in some ways I was more important than they were, as I had a new idea for them.

The man from Disney was certainly interested, or he would not have called me. The next step in the process was mine to make happen—but I did not even ask him for a meeting. For whatever reason(s), he decided to move on.

I dropped off a package for the Director of Operations at Paramount's Great America Park in Santa Clara, California. Later, I received a letter from him that said something along the lines of "Thank you for this information, but you did not answer several important questions or give us any information on some topics."

At the time, I took this letter to mean their answer was "no." These were "important" people and I did not want to bother them. They had told me "no," so I did not contact them again.

Years later, when I was older and smarter, I read the letter again. Then I kicked myself, because I realize now that the letter is not telling me "no." It actually says, "We are interested but your presentation doesn't tell us everything we need to know. Give us more information, please."

I had the amusement park in the technological center of the planet interested in my new technology system—and I did not follow up with them. I lost out on millions of dollars.

Mistakes

This story is presented here to help you learn from my mistakes. There were several:

- I thought these men were "smarter" than I was. They were not. They knew more about their parks, of course, but I knew more about my system. I needed to give them more information. Get a meeting with them. Explain it to them. Let them get comfortable with me. It takes time to get someone to buy your products/services, especially multi-million-dollar projects. I did not make the process happen.

  Nobody knows your product or offering better than you do. It is up to you to convey *whatever is necessary* to *whoever* is necessary in order to make your idea a reality. You will certainly talk with experts and "important" people who know more than you about their areas of expertise. However, nobody knows your new product or service as well as you do. You are the expert. Convey the required knowledge with enthusiasm and the important people will respond positively.

- I thought a simple "rejection" letter was the end of the line, when in fact it was an open invitation to provide more information.

- I did not get a patent for my system. The thought never occurred to me. Had I simply applied for a patent I would now have millions of dollars from Disney for use of my patented system. I could have licensed or sold them my patent, but I did not acquire one. I blew it.

  In my defense, I did not know anything about patents, except that they existed. You, however, now know that patents are very important and valuable. Do not make the same mistake I did by not patenting your idea. (See chapter on "Patents.")

- My desire was not strong enough to overcome the problems listed here. I knew I had a great idea, but I had not fanned the flames of desire for millions of dollars. I honestly was not even thinking much about money at the time, I just knew the idea was good. Since my desire was not strong enough, I faltered when I encountered the first bits of resistance.

- Further diminishing the chance of success, I had the wrong attitude in many ways and did not know the business process. My attitude was that I expected them to say no—why would they want to talk or work with me? So, when I heard anything "negative" I thought, "Ok, they said no. I should not bother them anymore."

This is completely the wrong attitude to have!

Bother them? I had a very cool, very useful state-of-the-art technology system (almost) ready for them. I had a way to make them vast sums of additional money and make their customers happier. It took them ten years until they finally implemented their own version of my system. Bother them? They were lucky I was calling!

But that is not what I thought at the time.

Learn from These Mistakes

Now *you* know this. Your million-dollar idea must be great and needed. It must be useful and beneficial to whoever is going to give you your million dollars. You are not bothering them; you are giving them something great! This is the attitude you will have, and this will guide your interactions with potential customers.

The Sales Process

At the time I was talking to the amusement parks, I did not know anything about the sales process. At first, the goal is not to sell something. At first, the goal is to keep people talking. How and why should there be another phone call? When can we have a meeting? It takes time to answer everyone's questions, get the right meetings, get the right approvals, get a contract developed, etc.

I was expecting a yes or no answer from the head of Disneyland on a first phone call, which is, of course, ridiculous.

After receiving my so-called (or so-thought) rejections, I gave up. I was on the right path but did not know it. I had a cool and extremely useful and beneficial product, some contacts with potential clients, and I did not continue as I should have done.

Live and Learn

There were some other reasons I did not acquire my million dollars with my line reservation system idea. Any one of them was enough to put me off the path to the money, and I had more than one issue.

My desire was not strong enough. While I thought I had a good idea and was excited by it, I did not have enough of a drive or passion about the idea to make it happen. I did not have a fixed amount of money in my head that I was determined to acquire. I was not driving towards something that I had to have.

My faith in myself was not strong enough. When you (incorrectly) think others are more important or smarter than you are, then you are at a disadvantage. I did not know how smart I was or realize how advanced I was with this idea. This has changed over time.

My faith in the process was not strong enough. I did not even know there was a process—either a general business process or the process discussed in this book of how to acquire a million dollars. If you have a good idea, desire, and passion, you follow the process and have faith in it, then it will get you to your million dollars.

Learn from these mistakes and pursue your idea and plans fervently. If you know your idea is good and your desire is strong, keep pushing until you are successful in bringing your million-dollar idea to the world. With the ride reservation system, I had what was certainly a *multi-million-dollar* idea—but I gave up on the pursuit of it for no good reason!

Fortunately, years later, I had another idea and I got it right.

Learn and Ask

"Of course, it was impossible to connect the dots looking forward when I was in college. But it was very, very clear looking backwards ten years later."

Steve Jobs (Founder of Apple Computer)

Silicon Valley entrepreneur and visionary Steve Jobs dropped out of college after six months. It was expensive and depleting his adoptive parent's life savings. However, he did not see how it would help him figure out what he wanted to do with his life, so he decided to follow his intuition and trust that everything would work out.

Years later, Stanford University asked him to give the commencement address at their graduation ceremony. He told the graduates (and subsequently millions of other people via online video sites) how dropping out was one of the best decisions of his life. However, after dropping out he did not leave campus. He attended only courses in which he was interested, rather than the required courses.

He took a calligraphy course and learned about fonts. It had no practical use in his life until ten years later when he was building an amazing, new computer. In 1984, the revolutionary Macintosh computer was the first to incorporate never-seen-before graphical fonts. They were the same fonts Jobs learned about after he dropped out of college.

"Of course, it was impossible to connect the dots looking forward when I was in college," he told the graduates, "But it was very, very clear looking backwards ten years later."

This story gives a clear message: *Learn about things in which you are interested. Learn everything you can.* You never know when something will be useful or beneficial to you.

Nobel Prize winning physicist Richard Feynman said it this way, *"Study hard what interests you the most in the most undisciplined, irreverent, and original manner possible."*

My Story

My connect-the-dots story is similar to Mr. Job's story, although the ending involves less money. Here are three separate "dots" from my life, events which later came together to help create a handheld GPS tour guide system:

- When I was 14 years old, I played on the school's teletype computer system. The computer printed out characters on a roll of paper—at ten characters per second. The games were simple but intrigued me. I wondered how they worked. I investigated and subsequently taught myself the BASIC computer language.
- When I was growing up, I learned to play an instrument. I played in any school band I could find and played

for any performance they gave. I joined the Minnesota State Youth Symphony and learned about classical music.

- Years later in New York City, I worked on the data and technical side of a "nearest store finder" project for a large telecommunication company. They wanted to know, for every person in the United States, which of the telecommunication company's stores was closest to their home address.

These three "dots" are each very different in subject and in the times in my life in which they took place. However, if you combine these three "dots"—you see the underlying framework for a handheld GPS tour guide system—which lead me to my million dollars:

First, the computer programming knowledge was directly useful in the system development. Second, I knew enough about music to make the tour content excellent (it even caused some Top of the Rock customers to cry!). Finally, the "nearest store locator" thinking is similar to how I solved the technical problem related to erroneous GPS signals caused by the concrete and steel canyons of New York City.

Just as Steve Jobs said, it was not clear to me going forward in my life how these dots would connect—but it is clear looking backwards how they came together to lead me towards my million dollars. Your million-dollar acquisition process will likely be a similar connect-the-dots story. *To maximize your chance for success you must learn as much as possible.*

More is Better

The more knowledge you have, the more "dots" you have. Any of them might connect you to your million dollars. For this reason, it makes sense to learn as much as you can, especially on topics that interest you.

Knowing as much as you can about as many topics as you can will yield other benefits in your life. You will be able to talk to more people about their expertise since you know something about their areas of knowledge. You will understand issues involved in many different areas, including business.

In business, you will know more about how many things work. This creates a better understanding of timing and costs, which helps minimize your costs in business negotiations. An unscrupulous person will not be able to take advantage of your lack of knowledge and charge you higher prices. You will also know more about what is and is not possible, which can prevent mistakes from happening.

Areas for Knowledge

You might want or need to learn in many areas in order to get you to your million dollars. Possibilities include:

- Software Applications

  Knowing the basics of many software applications is very helpful. Building websites, editing, and improving photographic images, videos, and sound files are very useful skills to know. They can come in handy when you are marketing your products or services. It is certainly possible to contract someone to do any work you need, and you should do so when you are short on time. However, it is nice to be able to have the capability to do some basic work yourself when you want something done in a moment's notice. (Possible software to learn how to use includes Photoshop, WordPress, Pro Tools, and Adobe's Premiere Pro).

- Manufacturing

  If your idea involves manufacturing a physical product, you should learn everything you can about production processes related to your idea. You might need to learn about metals or plastics if you are producing a solid product. You might need to learn about how food products are made in large quantities. There are many possibilities—the area in which you need to focus depends on your idea.

- Import/Export

  The import/export world has changed drastically in the last twenty years. It is now possible to buy a product from anywhere in the world and have it shipped to anywhere in the world. Costs and speeds of shipping have changed dramatically, too. Rules for imports and exports have changed, and tariffs are imposed and changed regularly. However, knowledge in this area might be very valuable to you. You will need to learn about import/export codes, what is and is not allowed, what value thresholds are taxed, etc.

- Biomedical Engineering/Biotechnology

  The human genome work of the last twenty years is beginning to pay off. The data humans can now collect about themselves is immense, and there is a huge possibility of drastic improvements in health associated with analysis of the data against rates of diseases. This field is going to be lucrative and experts are needed.

• Video Production

Huge changes in video delivery capability are creating the need for more and better video content. People with knowledge and skills in this field will be more and more valuable. Plenty of opportunities exist for men who learn these skills. Come up with new associated lucrative ideas and create new products and services based on those ideas.

These are just some of the areas in which a learned person should be able to create ideas and opportunities in the near future. Which of these topics are interesting to you? Is there something not listed which is more intriguing or appealing to you? Dive in and learn as much as you can on any topic that is interesting to you.

Some topics already have books and websites that have information about your subject. Other topics require a bit more research and only a few online videos might be available. Some topics might require discussions with a subject matter expert.

One thing you will find during your journey to your million dollars is that some people want to be helpful. You may find a serious subject matter expert who will be happy to help you. You simply have to ask them for assistance.

Learning from an Expert

One of America's great treasures, Stephen Sondheim was a creator of musical theater. You might not know his name, but you have likely heard some of his songs (e.g., "Send in the Clowns," which was a hit for Frank Sinatra, and "Everything's Coming up Roses" from the musical *Gypsy*). When he was in school, he asked Oscar Hammerstein—the lyricist of the world-famous *Sound of Music* show and movie, to critique a show that he wrote. This is a great example of asking for help from a subject matter expert. Hammerstein is one of the best ever.

Hammerstein told Sondheim that the show was the worst thing he had ever seen. Hammerstein then offered to spend an afternoon explaining to Sondheim why the show was bad. Reportedly, Sondheim later said, "In that afternoon, I learned more about songwriting and musical theater than most people learn in a lifetime." He learned from an expert.

Sondheim went on to create some of the most amazing work in Broadway history. One example: his *Sweeney Todd* turned into a blockbuster movie starring Johnny Depp.

Simply Ask

When Steve Jobs was twelve years old, he needed parts for a project on which he was working. He looked up the phone number of Bill Hewlett, the co-founder of the electronics company Hewlett-Packard (now known as "HP"). Hewlett not only gave Jobs the parts, he also gave Jobs a summer job at the Hewlett-Packard factory.

The parts and the summer job came to Jobs because he simply asked for some help. You can do the same thing. All you need to do is ask for help. You never know where it might lead. You might get what you ask for—and you might get something even better.

"Most people never ask, and sometimes that's what separates the people that do things from the people that just dream about them," said Jobs in a 1994 interview.

A Broadway Legend Who Asked for Help

Ask for expert help and you might land a job on Broadway!

Juliana Crawford moved to New York City in 2002 with dreams of working on Broadway. She had extensive experience working on national tours of Broadway shows, and now she was ready for the bright lights of Broadway. However, after a few years of trying, she had failed to obtain her Broadway debut.

She grew exasperated but did not give up. She wrote a letter to famed Broadway producer Hal Prince. Mr. Prince is not just any Broadway producer (if there is such a thing)—he has won more Tony awards than anyone else in history. He worked on *Cabaret, West Side Story, Sweeney Todd,* and *Phantom of the Opera.* Paraphrased, Ms. Crawford's letter said, "I have a ton of experience—what does a girl have to do to get a job in this town?"

A few days later, Ms. Crawford's phone rang. It was Hal Prince's secretary asking if Juliana Crawford wanted to come in for a meeting with Mr. Prince. She was surprised but managed to say, "Yes, of course!" A few days after that, Juliana Crawford was sitting at the desk of Broadway legend Hal Prince. All because she wrote a letter to a subject matter expert!

"I have a good feeling about you," Mr. Prince said. With that, he called the director of *Phantom of the Opera,* and Julianna landed her first Broadway job.

The story does not end there. Two years later, PBS filmed a documentary about Hal Prince. In the middle of the documentary Mr. Prince was asked, "When you first started sixty years ago—how did you get your first Broadway job?" His response was that he figured out who was the best/top Broadway producer—and he wrote a letter to him asking for help!

Learning and Help

The more knowledge you have, the better prepared you are to create, perform well, develop solid ideas and plans, execute plans, and save on costs. These are just a few of the benefits that come from having learned as much as possible.

With all of the information available on the Internet, there is no excuse for not learning about topics of interest to you. When the vastness of the Internet is not enough, you can request help from experts in your chosen fields. Many experts are willing to help if asked. In the process, you may pick up a summer job or a gig on Broadway—or something else that might be one of your "dots" on the path to your million dollars.

Learn as much as possible and ask for help. You never know what might happen.

Distractions and
Positive Questions

Nobel Prize winning author Ernest Hemingway kept a very strict schedule. Each day at 6 a.m., he climbed the wooden stairs of the secondary building behind his home in Key West, Florida. He entered and locked himself in with strict orders not to be disturbed. Then he spent the next six hours in his "office"—a beautiful room up in the palm trees, overlooking a swimming pool.

In his office, other than the view, there were no distractions. He could not click onto YouTube and watch a music video. He could not check what his friends were up to on Facebook. He could not go onto Twitter. He could not scroll through comments from people all over the world on whatever topic was distracting him.

He could, however, click on the manual keys of a typewriter that sat before him on a simple small, round table. In that spot, he knocked out some of the world's most famous novels.

He focused intently each day on his craft and made millions from it.

Do you want a million dollars? Do what successful people do and emulate Hemingway. Get rid of all the distractions in your life. You must focus on your idea and plan. It is not possible to focus too much on your idea and plan. Technology makes it too easy to be distracted—by a television news show, by the broadcast of a football game, etc. For the most part, you must banish distractions—especially (or at least) during your "working" time.

It takes intense focus to keep your conscious and subconscious mind trained on having the Universe deliver everything needed to obtain your million dollars. If you spend too much time on other things—too much time on worthless distractions—you are telling your brain and subconscious that the thing you said was important (your million dollars) is not that important. "Ok," it will respond, "then we don't have to spend the energy to make it happen."

It takes focus to think and create. To come up with your ideas. To come up with plans. To find the resources you need. To come up with more ideas. To market and sell your product, service, or whatever it is you are doing in exchange for your million dollars. If your focus is distracted, it disrupts the flow of creative energy needed to obtain the ideas and plans you need. It disrupts the flow of energy needed to execute your plans. Get rid of your distractions.

Despite being a data/technology expert who worked in Silicon Valley, I do not carry a cell phone. I rarely post on Facebook. I have never used Twitter. Unless you can use things in pursuit of your million dollars, you should not use them. They are huge wastes of time.

Action

Think through your daily activities. Think through everything you spend time doing. What things will help you get to your million dollars? Which things do nothing to help you towards your money? Are there actually things that set you back and push you away from your million dollars?

Banish anything that pushes you away from your millions. Then think through ways to minimize time spent on anything that does not advance you towards your million dollars. Implement any ideas you can to maximize the time you spend advancing towards your million dollars. Get rid of the distractions.

My Story

One evening in Charleston, South Carolina, I talked with a man who was interested in my background and the things on which I worked. My entrepreneurial experience was unusual in that town, so he started to pepper me with questions. We had a good and interesting conversation.

At one point he said, "I wish I could do something like that." I said, "You can, but you will have some problems."

"Like what?" he asked.

"Well, what did you do last night?" I asked.

"Oh, we went and watched the game at the sports bar across the street," he said, confirming my expectation.

"Last night, I taught myself how to operate some animation software," I told him. (At the time, I thought it might be useful. It turned out to be very difficult.) "Which is more useful to making money," I asked, "being in the sports bar or the software knowledge?"

He understood what I meant. Knowledge of animation software is much more likely to help someone make more money than having watched a football game.

The point is you decide what you do with your time. If you decide you want to distract yourself with a football game, that is your choice. However, it will not do much to help you acquire your millions. (Note: In general, software knowledge is more important. However, if you happen to be in a bar waiting to get a beer and you invent a new beer keg spigot that pours beer faster, you will make millions of dollars. Then going to the bar was a good idea.)

To acquire your million dollars, you must minimize your distractions.

Positive Questions

Similar to distractions, you must banish negative questions from your brain. Examine the difference in your thoughts to your answers to the following two questions:

Question One: Why have you not yet made a million dollars?

What are the reasons for you not making big money? You have not found the correct way to do it? You have not yet had time to do it? You are too hard at work at your current job?

Whatever the reason is, it is likely you have an answer or two to this question. The answers are satisfactory to you; you have a reason why you have not yet made your money.

Now examine your answer to this question:

Question Two: What things could you possibly do to make your million dollars or at least some extra money immediately?

Take a moment to come up with some answers to this second question.

When you have your answers, think about which question, one or two, is more likely to lead you to your million dollars. Which question is a positive question, and which is a negative one?

The first question does not really get you any closer to your million dollars. The only hope it has of helping is if you identify something that has been preventing you from earning your million dollars, and you can eliminate it. Otherwise, it is likely that the first question makes you more comfortable with *not* having a million dollars. You ask your brain the question and it gives you an answer. Since you came up with the answer, it must be a good one. Therefore, you have a "good reason" for not having a million dollars.

This is harmful to your accessing your million dollars. Not only does the question not get you closer to having your money, it actually makes you more comfortable with not having the money. Your answer gives you an excuse for not having the money, which makes you think it is not your fault you do not have the money. Since it is not your fault, there is nothing you can do about it. Therefore, you will not do anything about it.

To get your million dollars, it does *not* help to be comfortable with not having it! We have seen that money is energy and it flows to those that are ready for it and seek it. If you have a good reason for *not* having the money, then you are not ready for it. If you are not ready for it, it will not come to you.

Questions like Question One are distractions that will prevent you from acquiring your money. You need to banish questions like this one from spending time in your head. You must replace negative questions with positive ones.

Question Two is a positive one. It is the type of question to get you in the right frame of mind to reach your million dollars. It helps you focus on a way to get to your money.

What you focus upon is where you go! If you focus upon why you do *not* have a million dollars, then you will stay in that situation. If you focus on how to get to your million dollars, then you are heading in the right direction!

The questions you ask yourself have a *big* impact on your life. When you ask yourself a question you are telling your brain to focus on that question. If it is a negative question, then your life will stay negative. If you ask yourself helpful, positive questions, then you will see positive results.

Your brain responds to what you ask of it. If you ask yourself questions such as, "How do I improve this? How do I improve my situation? How do I make more money? How can I get a raise at work? How can I come up with a million-dollar idea?" and countless other positive questions you will achieve positive results.

Your subconscious feeds on what you put into it. If you fall asleep watching a worthless television show, you will likely have a worthless dream. If you fall asleep focusing on how to *solve* a business or life problem, then you might wake up in the middle of the night with a positive, life-altering idea.

It is good news that we can control our thoughts. Just a few paragraphs ago you focused on two different questions. You controlled the questions about which you thought. You can do this *at any time!* You can focus on positive questions if you choose to do so.

This means you have the ability to switch from negative thoughts to positive thoughts in an instant. Many people have never actively tried to do this, and it might take some getting used to doing it. However, you certainly have the ability to ask yourself questions that are more positive, and you have the ability to reduce and eliminate negative questions from your life.

By eliminating distractions and negative questions, you help your brain and subconscious focus on your plans and ideas. In this manner, you will join Hemingway, one of the most popular writers in American history, along with other millionaires.

Action

Begin to notice what types of questions you ask yourself on a daily basis. Every time you realize you have a question in your head, think about whether it is a positive or a negative question. Does it help you get closer to your million dollars? Or does it do nothing (or worse) to help you reach your goal?

If you encounter a negative question, actively change your thinking to a positive question. Possible alterations to your negative question include: "How do I solve this problem?" "What might be good about this situation?" or "How can I use this positively?"

For example, if nobody is returning your business phone calls, "Why does nobody call me back?" becomes "How do I get people to return my calls?" "Why can't I get any publicity for my business?" becomes "How do I get more publicity for my business?"

If these small changes seem silly to you, you do not yet fully understand how your subconscious works. You can direct your mind and subconscious to work on your problems for you. It will contact the Universe on your behalf and deliver to you answers to the questions you ask. So, make sure you are asking the right questions.

Patents and Trademarks

The television shows *Shark Tank* and *Dragon's Den* feature venture capitalists (VCs) that offer to buy percentages of aspiring entrepreneurs' companies. In the process, the VCs often ask the pitchman if he has a patent. This is a common question asked by venture capitalists. It is with good reason: patents can be very important and very valuable.

It is certainly possible to make your million dollars without obtaining a patent. Whether you need one or not depends on your business. It also depends on whether you have invented anything new and patentable.

The following gives you some information about trademarks, patents, the patent process, and what I went through to get my patent.

Trademarks

A **trademark** is a mark or symbol that identifies your products or services as coming from you. The famous "golden arches" of McDonald's is a trademark used by that company. No other company can use their logo. If someone does use the "golden arches" logo they can expect to hear from the intellectual property lawyers hired by the hamburger company.

If you have a logo, name, phrase, or something else that you want only your business to be able to use, you can register your item with the U.S. Patent and Trademark Office (USPTO). It is actual a fairly simple process. The uspto.gov website explains everything you need to know. They suggest you need a lawyer to assist you, but if you think you might not need a lawyer, then you probably will not need one.

In essence, the process requires that you enter your company information (or your name) and upload your logo (if that is what you want to trademark). You also tell them in which industry you plan to use the logo. You pay the filing fee (which is reduced if you do everything online) and that is it. Your logo is now officially registered. You can then use the special R inside a circle marking next to your logo or company name (if that is what you trademarked). Sometime later, you will receive an official record/booklet in the U.S. mail that shows your logo is trademarked.

How to Choose the Right Type of Patent

There are different types of patents. Which type is right for you depends on your invention. Unless you invent a new species of a plant, you only have to know about design patents and utility patents. Most likely, your invention will qualify for a utility patent, but first a few simple words about design patents.

Design patents are patents on the design or look of a product. For example, if you come up with an interesting new look for a shoe, you can try to receive a design patent. Obviously, you did not invent the "tool" or device that is a shoe—so you cannot receive a utility patent for the invention of the shoe. However, if your shoe looks somehow unique, this new design of shoe is patentable with a design patent. That way nobody can steal your new shoe design.

(Separately, you might put your company's logo on a new shoe. The shoe is not a new invention so you cannot patent it. However, like we discussed above, the logo can be trademarked as a special mark that belongs to you and your company. That way nobody can use your logo on a shoe or anything else.)

Another type of patent is a **utility patent**. This patent is granted to you if you invent a new machine, device, or even a system or method of doing something. In my case, I was the first person in the world to design, construct, and implement a GPS tour guide system for pedestrian use.

My invention was not a new piece of hardware or any type of device. My system used a preexisting handheld computer (or "personal digital assistant" as they were called at the time) combined with a GPS receiver that fit into the secure digital card slot of the PDA. For this reason, my patent is not for a new machine or new device.

Instead, I received my patent because I solved a problem with an existing system. The already patented vehicle-based GPS tour guide system would not work in New York City where I lived. Tall buildings interfere with the precision of the GPS signals, so the existing system would not function properly in NYC. One way to be awarded a patent is to invent something (a system or device) that fixes a known problem with an existing system or device. My invention did this, so I earned a U.S. patent—a utility patent, to be specific.

My Patent Story

The work for my GPS tour guide system required recording hundreds of audio files. My friend is a drummer and has a recording studio in New York City, so he was the obvious choice to do the work.

On more than one occasion, he said to me, "You really should get a patent for this." It seemed a little silly to me, since to me the GPS tour guide was an "obvious" invention. One of the requirements for obtaining a patent is that your invention is "non-obvious." So, I was not sure if my invention qualified for a patent.

However, one day I decided to research patents. It turned out there were other patents in the same field as mine. In fact, there was one titled "Position Responsive, Hierarchically-Selectable Information Presentation System and Control Program." This patent was for a GPS tour guide system just like mine, except for use in vehicles. (Interestingly, it did not belong to the man who started GoCar GPS tours in San Francisco.) My system was for pedestrian use, which was an important distinction.

From this I concluded that my system was patentable. However, I still hesitated for many reasons. I did not know how to get a patent, and it seemed like it would require a lot of work. It would take up a lot of time—and there was no guarantee that it would be of any value. I put the idea of getting a patent on the back burner. I decided that maybe I would work on it later.

However, my subconscious was already at work. I told it that this was an important topic and needed an answer. The idea about the patent soon popped back into my head. "OK, what do I need to get a patent?" I asked myself.

I knew there were patent lawyers who I could pay for help. But I also knew they were expensive. You can easily pay one over $20,000 to file a patent for you. I did not like that idea.

Meanwhile I thought, "Patent lawyers did not used to exist. You used to be able to get a patent without their help. The U.S. Patent system is the same system it always has been, so I should be able to get a patent without a patent lawyer. How do I do this?"

This led me to quite a bit of reading about patents and patent lawyers. I found helpful information on the U.S. Patent and Trademark Office website (uspto.gov). Then I read and studied many patent documents to see how they were written and what information was contained in them.

Eventually I saw patterns in the documents and how they were constructed. Since these were real patents that were accepted by the U.S. Patent Office, I knew if I wrote my patent in a manner similar to them that my patent would have a chance of being accepted (or "allowed," to use the same term that the patent office uses. They "allow" you to patent your invention).

That is what I did. I "modeled" my patent document to look like and sound like a patent that already existed. I copied the style, tone, and format of the existing patents. I wrote new material that explained how my invention worked and placed it into my new patent document at the appropriate places. I replaced the material that explained the previous patent document's invention with my explanation of my invention. This made sense to me and worked out well.

Solve a Problem—Get a Patent

To solve the GPS interference problem, I spent hours running around Manhattan with a handheld computer and a GPS receiver—measuring where the device worked well and where it did not.

I got a "feel" for how good (or bad) the GPS signals were in NYC and realized a GPS tour guide system would work, but not the same way as the vehicle-based system. The vehicle-based system says, "OK, you are here, so you need to hear this information." Because the GPS signals are not perfectly accurate in NYC, this system will not always deliver the correct information in NYC or any other location with tall buildings, large trees, etc.

My pedestrian-based system says "OK, you are somewhere around here, you should select the appropriate information from this list." The system bases the list on where the GPS system thinks you are located. Finally, because in NYC, where the GPS thinks you are is always "close enough" to where you actually are, the list includes the point-of-interest in front of which you are standing. Problem solved.

Since I solved a problem with a previous patent, my new system was patentable. All I had to do to receive a patent was document the system in a patent application and submit it to the Patent Office of the United States of America.

Writing Your Patent

By the time I decided to file for a patent, I already had a working GPS tour guide business in New York City. I wrote the tour guide script for all of the points-of-interest (over 300). I recorded the MP3 files. I selected and/or created appropriate .jpg photos and videos for each point-of-interest. I mapped the locations of most of the subway entrances in NYC. I determined their latitudes and longitudes. I had NYC themed music ready in the software. I did many things and had started the business, renting GPS tour guide devices to tourists.

Finally, I turned my attention to writing a patent. I visited the U.S. Patent and Trademark website (uspto.gov) and the Google Patents website. After I investigated types of patents, the tone, style of the writing, etc., I finally thought, "OK, I am going to write my own patent application."

I took a large legal pad with me and walked to the now long-gone NY Film School Cafe. I sat outside the cafe and watched people walk from St. Mark's Street to Astor Place while I made notes as to what would be in my patent. Then, I went to my apartment and used a computer to convert the notes into more coherent content for the patent application.

This process of thinking, writing, and reviewing existing patents went on for approximately two months. I did not work on it for 40 hours per week, but it took some time each week and most days. When I finished, I remember thinking, "OK, I saved $20,000, but maybe I should have spent that money on a lawyer to save me the work and time I had to put in." I felt like I had done a significant amount of work, and I understood why lawyers charge money to do the work.

Then, I would remind myself that I had to write most of the material myself anyway, as there was no way a lawyer would know all the details of my system. In my situation, I felt like I had to do much of the work myself anyway, so why pay a whole patent application fee to a lawyer? Of course, now that it is complete, even years later, I am happy and proud that I did it myself.

Wait and Receive

One of the last things I did when writing my patent was decide what to call my system. This would be the title of my invention—and the title of my patent application. My system was a GPS tour guide system, to be sure, but it was more than that. Since the system can be used for any type of information, not just tourist information, I broadened the scope of my patent request a bit and titled my patent "Location-based Information Delivery System for Pedestrian Use." (You can view the patent by searching for this title in

Google, Google Patents, or better yet, at the U.S. Patent and Trademark website at uspto.gov)

When I finished writing the application, I used the online system to upload and submit the required material. I paid the fees. I hit "submit" and received notification that my submission was received by the U.S. Patent and Trade Organization. Then I waited.

I waited for three years.

One day, three years later, my telephone rang. The caller identification screen said the call was from the "U.S. Patent and Trademark Office." "Wow," I thought as I answered the phone.

The helpful and intelligent man from the patent office explained to me that they could not approve my patent as submitted. The good news was that I already knew many patents are initially rejected for various problems, so I was not surprised or unhappy with this information. In fact, since I wrote the application myself, I knew there was a higher likelihood there could be a problem.

The man from the U.S. Patent Office suggested changes that I did not quite understand, but I took some notes. I told him I would resubmit an updated application as soon as possible. I made changes to my application and hit the submit button once again.

This time I waited six months until the phone rang. The same man called and told me he had my updated application. "Great!" I told him. Then there was a long pause.

"It looks like you don't know what you are doing," he finally said.

I laughed and said, "That is correct."

This made him happy. I have spent countless hours around engineers—and sometimes this type of "straight talk" is required. Some people would take what he said to me as an insult. But I was not offended by what he said to me, because it was the truth. By admitting to him I did not know what I was doing when I made the changes, he was free to tell me what I did wrong. More importantly, he decided he would help me.

"Tell you what," he said, "I'm going to suggest a few changes to you now over the telephone. I will record the conversation. You agree to the changes, and I will allow your patent." "Ok!" I responded. I was not sure what "allow your patent" meant, but he was clearly trying to be helpful.

One of the sticking points was that I had apparently tried to put too much into my system. I realized that the content I was going to deliver to GPS tour guide users could come from their handheld device or delivered from a computer at another location (e.g., a "cloud" computer). The patent examiner said that was two different inventions, so we took out the part about the cloud computer content.

He then quickly made a few additional suggestions on what information to change, delete, and in which section some of the material should be placed. I agreed to each of his suggestions. Finally, he said, "OK, now I will allow your patent." It turned out this meant he was granting me the patent.

My life changed forever. I was officially an inventor.

A month later, I received a large envelope from the U.S. Patent Office. It had the official booklet copy of my patent. It is a simple booklet. The cover is a bit fancier than the rest of the document. The rest is just plain paper. However, it is the official record of my being awarded a patent by the United States Patent Office.

Soon after the patent was issued, I started receiving solicitations in the mail to purchase fancier versions of the patent award document. Independent companies mail official looking papers that say, "Send us $150, and we will send you a wooden plaque version of your patent award document." If you want a fancy version of your patent hanging on your wall, this is the way to go. Do not expect anything too fancy from the patent office, although the booklet is a nice reminder of the accomplishment.

To Sell Your Patent or Not

Nothing immediately changed in my life after I received my patent. I continued efforts to rent the GPS devices to tourists. I continued to work on data analysis projects.

But one day in my occasional Google research, I found new information about the patent for the vehicle-based GPS tour guide system. It was sold at a technology auction. With more research, I found that the patent sold for one million dollars!

This got my attention.

I had wondered if I would ever want to sell my patent. It did not interest me... until I saw it might be worth one million dollars! "OK," I thought, "I would sell my patent for one million dollars!"

The next day, I researched the company that ran the auction. I sent them an email. My email told them I had a patent very similar to the one they sold at their earlier auction—and I asked them if they would be interested in selling mine.

Four hours later, my phone rang. It was a man who made over $50 million in technology, retired early, then got bored and started the technology/intellectual property auction company. "I'm the guy who sold the patent you mentioned in your email," he told me, "and I can sell yours, too."

He also told me he would send me the paperwork. An hour later, his assistant emailed me the simple forms. All I had to do was sign the forms, and they would try to sell my patent at their next auction.

This made me nervous. Was I going to sign away the rights to my invention? Who was this man? Was this company legitimate?

I researched the company and the man that started it. That is how I discovered he made $50 million in the cell phone industry. I decided a man with $50 million did not need to steal my patent, so I filled out the forms and mailed them to the company. I agreed to sell my patent at a technology auction to be held a few months later in Silicon Valley.

The Sale

Before the auction, I received phone calls from interested companies that had questions about my patent. Mostly they wanted to make sure I actually had the rights to the patent "free and clear" of anyone else that I might have worked with at any time.

The auction was at the Ritz-Carlton hotel in San Francisco, high atop Nob Hill. Outside, cable cars passed by on California Street. Inside, millions of dollars of patents waited to be sold. I was given an invitation and a ticket, but I did not attend the event.

At the time of the event, I sat at my desk in my apartment in Greenwich Village, NYC. I found an attendee using Twitter to "broadcast" the auction results. My patent was the first one on the auction block because it was one of the more exciting ones. The auctioneers wanted to start the event with a good, solid, exciting sale.

A few minutes after the auction began, I found a tweet on Twitter... that said my patent had sold for $615,000. About an hour later, I received an email from the auction company confirming I had just made a lot of money.

Just like that, I had a half-million dollars.

I called my parents and told my father, "My patent sold, but I did not get a million dollars for it." He laughed, as he thought I was joking when I said my patent might sell for that much money. "But," I continued, "I did get a half-million dollars." He did not laugh. "Oh really?" he said, clearly shocked. He could not believe it.

Why is it Valuable?

A patent gives you the exclusive rights to use your invention. If anyone else uses or copies your system, method, or device they are infringing on your rights. Your options then are to license the use of the patented system to them or sue them for infringement of your patent. In either case, you will earn money if indeed they are infringing on your patented system or device.

That is why a patent is valuable. Having one means anyone who uses your invention must pay you money.

In my case, through the auction, I sold the rights to my patent to a law firm that specializes in patent law. The company will likely contact many companies whose software and systems violate my patent. Either the law firm will license the use of my patented system to the companies, or the law firm will sue the companies for infringement. Both outcomes will yield payouts to the law firm. In effect, the money I received was front money for licensing my patent.

What About You?

Have you invented something? Get a patent. All of the required information on how to acquire one is available at the U.S. patent website (uspto.gov).

My patent story might make it seem like it is easy to receive a patent. In some ways it is. The process is straightforward. However, it is a lot of work to develop the written material for the patent, put it into the correct format, deal with the patent office, make any required changes, and receive the patent.

Since I am not a lawyer, none of the material contained in this chapter should be considered legal advice. However, I hope it is beneficial to you to know that I wrote my own patent without a patent lawyer. I received a patent for my invention without assistance from anyone other than the patent examiner.

By Yourself or Get Help?

If you are an analytical person, good at things like mathematics, engineering, and computer programming, you are a good candidate to navigate the patent process successfully on your own. If you are more of a "creative" artistic type, good at drawing, colors, and design, you might want to get some help with the patenting process.

If you already have $20,000 to pay a patent lawyer, you should consider that route, especially if your available time is limited.

On the other hand, if you have time available and do not want to or cannot spend money for a patent lawyer, it is possible to write and receive a patent without the help of a patent lawyer. Nothing prevents you from trying on your own.

The U.S. Patent and Trademark Office is there to assist you in the process of obtaining your patent or trademark. The patent and trademark system exists to give you some protection for your hard work and ideas.

Stocks—What to Do with Your Million Dollars

O nce you have your million dollars, you need to know what to do with it. There are plenty of books, videos, and other resources that give financial advice.

The good news is that once you accumulate enough money you can use it to "work" for you while you sleep. The money (energy) can return more money to you. In some cases, it will arrive "slowly but surely," and, in other cases, it will arrive quickly.

Some of the money I have earned is from wise stock investments. Because I have had success, I will pass my thoughts on the topic along to you.

The Playing Field—The Short-Term Game

I recommend you do *not* try to be a "day trader" in stocks. Buying and selling stocks the same day to try to "catch" a short-term trend is difficult. Making money by "timing" stock prices is almost impossible for the average investor.

The "Big Guys" on Wall Street have a lot more money to invest than you do. They are also looking to make money as fast as possible. Some of them are trying to make millions of dollars in *seconds*, which is something you probably never thought was possible.

(Example: There is a building in New York City just north of Wall Street. Companies are positioning their computers physically closer to this building because it is the end of a computer wire coming from Chicago. The microsecond advantage they have by having their computers closer to the information flowing from Chicago allows them to buy "low" and immediately sell "high" for a fraction of a penny advantage. This tiny fraction yields guaranteed money—and at high volumes yields large sums of money)

Fortunately, you do not need to go up against the Wall Street guys. They have the best computers, the best systems, the best inside information, the best algorithms, and the best lawyers. You cannot compete with them.

A man with Russian contacts was arrested for stealing a computer algorithm from Goldman Sachs, the huge investment-banking firm. A spokesman from Goldman Sachs said at the time (paraphrased), "This is a major theft—with this algorithm the Russians could manipulate the U.S. markets!" This meant, of course, that Goldman Sachs could manipulate the U.S. markets.

You do not have such power and cannot compete against these firms. So, in most cases a "short-term" stock buying and selling strategy is not a good idea.

Short Term—The Disaster Strategy

While you cannot compete against the Wall Street firms, there are ways to use what they do to your advantage. One possible method to employ is my "Disaster Strategy."

An Oil Spill Opportunity

On April 20, 2010, a huge oil spill occurred in the Gulf of Mexico. An oil rig owned by BP (British Petroleum) dumped huge amounts of oil into the water. At the time, their stock was trading at almost $60 per share. A few days later, as word about the size of the disaster started to leak out—the stock price began to tank.

Two weeks later, the stock was down 15%. Two weeks after that, it was down 20%. A total of eight weeks later, it was down almost 50%.

According to the stock market, the company had lost half of its value. Was this possible? Was the company really worth half of what it was just a short time earlier? Was the damage to BP half of their company?

At the time it was clear that the U.S. government would fine the company, as it does every time there is an environmental disaster. It was also clear the disaster was a large one. It turned out to be the biggest U.S. oil spill in history.

Here is where my stock "disaster strategy" came into play.

I researched and found the largest U.S. fine assessed for a previous oil spill. Then I added ten percent to that figure, since I assumed (correctly) that the U.S. government would increase the amount of the fine from the previous record. I took that number and calculated what percentage of BP's company value (market capitalization) that figure represented.

That told me roughly how much damage the oil spill was going to cause to the company's financial situation. The percent damage to the company's value, in my estimation, was going to be about five percent. But the stock price had gone down first ten, then twenty, thirty, forty, fifty percent. The market, dominated by the "big guys" who are focused on short-term impact on prices, had driven down the BP stock price way below where it was going to end up when the dust settled.

I was fortunate to have some cash sitting in a bank account at the time. I took the subway up to a financial office on Park Avenue in New York City and handed them the biggest check I had written in my life. They deposited the cash into my stock/brokerage account, and I used all the money to buy BP stock. Then I waited.

It took some time to cap the oil leak. They assessed the damage, and the stock price began to rebound. The company was fined almost exactly what I predicted, and I made approximately thirty percent on my investment in six months. Once the stock price hit my calculated value, I sold it. The stock stayed at that price for the next three years.

Of course, the "Disaster Strategy" approach is not foolproof, but there is some sound reasoning and calculations behind it. You can add it to your toolkit for stock selection.

There is never a "sure thing" in stock investing. However, I felt very confident that my calculations and logic were sound when I wrote the check to the financial company. The reward for my research and calculations was a nice profit a few months later.

Long Term—Value Strategy

Since the "big guy" investors focus on short-term gains, other investors can increase their wealth by buying stocks that take a little longer to increase in value. To understand which stocks will grow, you need to understand what a stock price represents and why it goes up.

The best explanation of the basics of stock investing comes from Warren Buffett. He gives an example about a man who starts a gumball machine business.

The man places ten gumball machines at various locations in town and profits about $1,000 per month from the machines. This is $12,000 per year. However, the man tires of the business and offers to sell it to you.

How much would you pay for the business that generates $12,000 per year in profits? What is the value of this business?

If you pay him $12,000, then after one year you will have earned your investment back. After two years you will have your original $12,000 plus another $12,000. So, you would be up $12,000, and you still own the business. That would be a 100% return on your investment in two years (and you still own the business).

However, the man says $12,000 is not enough to buy this (almost) guaranteed income of $12,000 per year. Eventually you settle on $36,000 as the price you pay him for the business. You now own 100% of the business, for which you paid $36K. In stock market speak, the "market capitalization" for this gumball business is $36,000, because the "market" paid $36K for the entire business. That is the total value of the company according to the market.

You take over the business and get to work. You expand the business into another town, which quickly generates another $1,000 per month in profit. Now, if you wanted to sell the business you could easily justify a price of $72K, since the profit has doubled. And if you wanted to sell, you could also point out how easy it was to expand into the new town—and point to neighboring towns in which you could expand—showing that the business is worth potentially much more than $72K.

In this example, you bought 100% of the company. When a company issues stock, they sell only a portion of the company and keep the rest for themselves. If they sell 50% of the company, for example, and you bought all of the stock, you would pay $18K for 50% of the company (since you agreed the entire company was worth $36K). The company can say you own as many shares as they wish, but they must delineate what percentage of the company your shares represent.

As the company grows and/or shows they can expand further, the value of the company—and therefore the value of your shares—increases. The more the company shows they can expand and grow, the more your shares of the company are worth.

Picking a Stock on Value

If you can find a company that is likely to grow and expand, it stands a good chance that the value of the company (and therefore the price of its stock shares) will increase. If you own stock in such a company, your wealth will increase over time.

Recent examples of such stocks that had good long runs with price increases include Starbucks, Federal Express, and Netflix. All of these companies delivered strong value to their customers, and each had plenty of room to expand and grow. As they did, the price of their stock increased.

Starbucks started in Seattle and, after trial-and-error, finally arrived at a successful "formula" for a store. Then, they expanded across the U.S. and the world. Their stock priced doubled every three years for approximately 25 years. This means if you invested at any point during this 25-year stretch you would have doubled your money every three years. That is a very good rate of return.

In 1998, people started using the Internet for online shopping. Most online purchases need to be delivered by a shipping company. At the time, Federal Express was uniquely positioned with the best technology to handle the new shipping business. Just as the value of the gumball business increased when new cities became available, the value of FedEx increased when a new market was created for it. Twenty years later their stock price has quadrupled.

In 2008, Netflix was having great success with its movie delivery service. Since the business is scalable to the entire world—not just local cities for gumball delivery—the stock price skyrocketed. In 2008, the share price was $4. In 2018, it reached $400 per share. If you bought $1,000's worth of stock in 2008, you would now have $100,000. If you had bought $10,000's worth, you would now have your million dollars!

Be on the Lookout

These examples suggest it is possible to make money in the stock market with a longer-term value approach. To do so, you must be "on the lookout" for stock purchasing opportunities. If you discover a company with a good product that you understand—and see that it has clear opportunities for growth—it might be a good company in which to invest.

How do you know for sure the stock price will go up? You do not and you never will. However, you need to invest in something in order to have your money earn money for you. If your money sits in a bank earning almost no interest, the money will not help you increase your wealth—and in fact, you will *lose* purchasing power as prices increase. If you invest your money in opportunities for growth and expansion, your money/energy can grow for you.

Technology Opportunities

Your million-dollar idea may or may not leverage technology as a key component. However, since changes produce opportunities and there have been many changes in the technological world in the last two decades, devoting a few pages here to technological opportunities may be of benefit.

There are a few places to look to make money today using technology. In order to understand where to look—and why—it helps to look at technological advances in the last 25 years. This helps you understand where changes took place and anticipate where they will happen next.

The 1980s, 90s and 2000 (Computers and the Internet Arrive)

Personal computers started to appear in households in the 1980s. These devices went to work doing basic word processing and simple financial analysis in a spreadsheet program. There were a few computer games with very basic graphics. The famous Macintosh "1984" commercial aired in 1984 and launched the first "talking" computer with graphics.

Netscape programmer Marc Andreessen invented the first commercial Internet browser in 1994. It made him very rich. It took five years until people started buying things online in large quantities. The first generic reusable web-based storefront company launched in 1995 and sold to Yahoo! in 1998 for $49 million. The first man to sell large quantities of books online named his company Amazon. It is now worth billions.

The online commerce platform sale to Yahoo! and the development of Amazon are just two examples of men taking advantage of advancements in computer and Internet technology to make millions of dollars. By monitoring changes and their associated opportunities, you can do the same. However, you must be looking for the opportunities, and you must act on them.

The growth of the Internet drew the attention of venture capitalists who saw chances to make quick money. A sort of "gold rush" ensued, with investors clamoring to put their money into "online stocks." Stocks in Internet companies skyrocketed in value, while the underlying financial situations of many of the Internet companies did not. A large stock market crash started in 2000, following the "dot-com bubble." This led to the liquidation of many "up-and-coming" Internet companies.

The Dot-Com Crash

There were several losers in the dot-com market crash in the year 2000. Most famously was a website called Pets.com. The site sold items for pets.

It is important to note that today there are many websites from which you can buy cat food, dog food and other pet-related items. So, the idea of selling pet food online was and still is a good one.

Why then did Pets.com, the first big player in the marketplace, go out of business? The simplest answer is that they ran out of cash. Their expenses were too great compared to their income. It cost too much to develop all of the software that they needed (much of the software that is available cheaply now was not available then) and the online marketplace was nowhere near as large as it is now. High costs plus too little income led to a crash of the company. (A case can also be made that venture capitalists were going for quick online money rather than building and developing companies.)

This story should act as a cautionary tale to those that wish to "get rich quick." As the dot-com bubble grew, enamored (and suddenly wealthy) investors treated one advertising CEO like a rock star. A year later, his company went bankrupt, and anyone left holding shares of stock in the company saw their value go to zero.

After the dot-com crash, many people said it was the end of the Internet, online commerce, and especially of "online advertising." This, of course, was wrong.

Online Growth

Facebook started in 2003 and became available to everyone in 2006. The video service YouTube started in 2005. Since these sites allowed users to spend an indefinite amount of time on them, people began to spend more time on the Internet. The average amount of time spent online per person in the U.S.A. (and around the world) increased greatly. Since people spent more time "online," it made sense that advertising would follow them.

Facebook, YouTube, and many other companies sold advertising opportunities to marketers, the first of which saw large returns on their marketing investments. It paid off to be an early adopter of the new advertising opportunities. The payoff diminished as more people used the services and prices for advertising increased dramatically.

Who Else Made Money?

Companies that produced software that served advertising made money. Companies that created and produced the advertisements made money. Many of these companies were bought by larger companies, making additional money for the workers and founders of the original companies.

Wanting to encourage creators of videos, YouTube started sharing advertising dollars with content creators, which yielded a handful of "YouTube Stars" who made millions of dollars from the advertising shown in conjunction with their videos.

In 2007/2008, programmers could sell games and other applications online for the new Apple iPhone. The first movers made simple games and made large piles of money in short time spans (days/months). In 2009, a Finnish company released a game called "Angry Birds." It was more complex than the original games, but still simple. It made the creators millionaires and spawned a full-length movie. These examples show how first movers in technology made money in the last two decades.

Recent Changes and the Future

The changes in technology, infrastructure, and the marketplace of the past twenty years created opportunities that did not exist just years earlier. Some of these opportunities have come and gone. Changes have also created opportunities that exist now and will exist in the near future. It is worth examining a few changes to see how they played out and how they will affect the future.

First, the initial fervor about the Internet is in the past. The "wow, I need to have this" fever—which accompanied personal home computers (PCs), the Internet (see America Online) and then the iPhone (which connected easily to the Internet) is already a thing of the past.

Second, hardware "must haves" fueled much of the technology boom of the 1990s and 2000s. The PC became a household item in the 1980s and 1990s. Many people made money in the process (see University of Texas student Michael Dell). The Internet cranked into high gear thanks to Netscape's browser in 1995. Online sales began in earnest soon after that. In 2007, the iPhone debuted, so today people wander the streets with access to the Internet in their pocket. Today these hardware items are ubiquitous, whereas not too long ago they were novelties.

Online commerce has increased enormously. The number of purchases made using the Internet has increased tremendously since the dot-com era. Ideas for online businesses that were not feasible before are feasible now.

Another major change is that bandwidth has increased for both mobile use and at-home cable Internet speeds. Speeds will continue to increase. Today, people watch videos online and listen to music with clarity and speed never seen before. The upcoming 5G (Fifth Generation) mobile devices increase Wi-Fi/Internet speeds approximately ten times. This will make it possible to view video, and in general move more data, over mobile devices than in the past.

So Where Are We Now?

These major and rapid technological changes bring us to the current state:

- Everyone has the Internet in their hand.
- Everyone uses mobile Internet devices.
- Everyone buys things online.
- People are spending more time online.
- Bandwidth has greatly increased. (In 1995 we shared basic text files on the Internet, now we share videos and real-time video via applications like Skype or Periscope.tv.)
- Production of content (specifically video) is cheap—and more people have the capability.
- Anyone can broadcast (Periscope.tv, Facebook Live, etc.).

If you want to make money now by taking advantage of these changes, the question to ask yourself is, what impact will these changes have? What opportunities do these create?

The changes listed above yield opportunities in many areas, including software applications, news and information delivery, niche ecommerce websites, and video and other online content production. A few words on each of these topics is below.

Application Opportunities

The hardware, software, and technology infrastructure opportunities of the 1980s, 1990s, and 2000s have been surpassed by opportunities in the application of the technologies. The Internet infrastructure is in place. The opportunities are now in *using* the infrastructure.

This is why Google and Facebook opened additional headquarters in New York City. Silicon Valley is very important and full of hardware and software ideas, but the next phase of opportunity is in new applications of the recently built technology infrastructure.

Hollywood has the best movie production capabilities in the world; New York City has solid television production and is the world center of many media operations (including CBS, NBC, Fox News, the *New York Times*, and many other outlets). It is also home to the world headquarters of many other major companies. Now that the Internet has become so important to the world's commerce and communication, it makes sense that major technology players (IBM, Facebook, and Google) open headquarters in NYC. The growth of Silicon Valley in the past two decades will be matched or surpassed by other industries making similar advances. They will use the technology provided by Silicon Valley. To aid, influence, and make money from them, many technology companies are moving to New York City.

Companies and other businessmen can act on this knowledge to take advantage of the changes. There are opportunities for anyone who wants to facilitate development of corporations that seek to use the new infrastructure. Entertainment, online commerce, and other areas are all ripe for advancements.

Questions to ask include "How can we assist major companies to take advantage of the technology infrastructure?" or possibly better yet, "How can we blow out existing major companies by taking advantage of new technology?" (Remember, your author, working out of a small apartment in Manhattan, had a better product—one that actually worked—than the vaunted or venerable Microsoft Corporation.)

Some areas now undergoing transformation in which people with good ideas can take advantage of opportunities include:

- News and Information

Information dissemination—who do you trust for news about an event? Do you rely on a single newspaper, or would you prefer to see multiple videos from the event itself so you can judge what happened? The advancements of video and communication have developed opportunities for news and information websites. News organizations that have had monopolies for years over what the people see and hear no longer have a monopoly on reporting. There are large opportunities for news- and information-delivery applications and systems.

- Video Editing

The area of video editing and production is hot right now. Sixteen-year-old "children" are making $100 per hour editing videos. Simple editing software is available for free. People who do not know how to use the technology and/or do not have the time to do the work pay for video editing services.

While video editing as a business is somewhat limited to a "pay per hour" service, the sixteen-year-olds who are making $100 an hour certainly feel like millionaires when they compare themselves to classmates who are making minimum wage.

- Niche Websites

The success of Amazon can be used against it. If someone wants a specific item, the search function on Amazon is great. However, if someone wants to browse and shop for "random" items—it is terrible. There are too many items and too much clutter. People like simplicity and ease. They would prefer to shop on a site that caters to their specific interests. It would be much nicer if a website had only things the customer likes. That is why opportunities exist for niche sales websites.

Online shopping is "regular" shopping now, with a few very important differences. One of them is that *anyone* can open a store and sell things online. The software is now commonplace. Sure, you can sell through an already existing store (e.g., eBay, Amazon), but it is also possible to create your own store and sell very specific products, which all have "affinities" with each other. That means someone who buys one item is likely to buy one of the other items—and for the customer it means it will be easier to find items in which they are interested. Both the seller and the customer will be happier.

As an example, a niche online store could sell books and videos about artists or music or one specific genre of music—e.g., a music shop that only sells 1950s doo-wop music—or 1970s and 1980s rock-n-roll music. It would be very easy to create an online store that sells 1950s music and then replicate the site/system, creating another site that sells 1960s music, another that sells 1970s music, etc.

For years, the "Time Life" company sold nostalgia. Their books, records, and videos sold millions, and there is a reason for it. (However, Time Life's original attempt at selling the same content on the Internet was called "Pathfinder," and it failed spectacularly, similarly to Pets.com failure but without the venture capital component.) Nostalgia for the past is a strong emotion. Online commerce websites targeted at appropriate niches could tap into this emotion and market.

Another niche is pure content sites—each serving a special niche. Videos with a particular slant (political, humor, historical, pets, cats, dogs, etc.) could be sold and/or "broadcast" with advertising opportunities generating revenue. A hybrid website could integrate articles, photos, and videos that create nostalgia—and supply plenty of online commerce opportunities.

Opportunities exist for those who seek them. Be on the lookout for something that is appropriate for you.

Content is King Again

Whatever the focus of someone's website, it needs good content. With more people and more companies producing more websites, there is a need for more and better content. A clearinghouse of articles and a production company for videos should be able to find opportunities for paid work.

Meanwhile, as a business, direct-to-consumer video delivery will become easier. Costs of production and delivery are coming down, and the ease-of-use of server software is increasing. Video producers who deliver their own content and own advertising, if they wish, can keep the lion's share of the revenue generated by the content. There will be no need for YouTube to take a percentage cut from the total revenue.

In the past, if you wanted to produce a movie, you had to hope for a deal with Hollywood. The movie moguls there had the equipment and resources to produce movies. They still do, but they are being joined by Netflix, Amazon, and other companies producing and selling their own content. There is nothing to stop smaller players from replicating and surpassing the movie moguls and well-backed companies—at least on a per-movie basis. If you are a small business, all you need is one giant success to become wealthy—and to propel yourself into being a medium- or larger-sized business.

Other Technology Opportunities

The changes and opportunities discussed here are certainly not an exhaustive list. There are many other opportunities related to technology that will make men millions of dollars. While there has been much focus on the Internet for the past two decades, other creations, including a handheld GPS tour guide system, did not use the Internet.

What you work on will depend on your background, knowledge, thoughts, ideas, contacts, and focus. It may or may not depend largely on technology—but there are certainly opportunities in technology for those that want to pursue them.

Controlling Your Thoughts

There is a path available to you that leads you to your million dollars. It is up to you to decide if and when you will travel down the path. Notice, this choice is completely up to you. Either you decide you will do it and take action—or you do not take action, effectively deciding not to take the path and not to have a million dollars.

Along the way, there may be obstacles. Some of them, especially at the beginning, are simply thoughts in your head. They may slow you down, but by controlling your thoughts, you can ignore some of them. Remember, you decide what remains in your head for any length of time. You control your thoughts.

What you think about has a huge impact on your life. There are consequences that stem from your thoughts. Some thoughts propel you towards success; some thoughts prevent you from making any progress. These latter thoughts are obstacles. You must overcome them before you can succeed.

Thoughts as Obstacles

It is possible that your thoughts are preventing you from achieving the success of acquiring your million dollars. For some people, the maxim "you are your own worst enemy" is true.

Let us look at it this way: If you already had a few million dollars and somehow somebody stole all of the money from you, would you be upset? Of course you would! You would want to track down the thief and put him in jail (or worse)!

But what if the thief is you?

If your thoughts are preventing you from obtaining your million dollars, then *you* are stealing from yourself! You are preventing your million dollars from being in your possession.

Your thoughts can rob you of your million dollars in multiple ways. Two are discussed below. The good news is that you control your thoughts. This means *you* can avoid or stop the bad thoughts from causing the theft. It is up to you.

Theft by Paycheck

You control your thoughts. If you are going to work every day to make some money, you have effectively given away time for thinking about making a million dollars in exchange for the safety of a relatively small regular paycheck. This seems nice unless or until the company goes out of business or "lays off" workers—which companies can do at any time.

Notice that if you are doing this, your thoughts about the importance of safety are preventing you from spending that time pursuing your million dollars. When you are at work, instead of focusing on acquiring your million dollars, you focus on whatever your boss tells you is important. You have ceded a large portion of your time to a company. This means someone else is making money off your time.

While you are at your job collecting a paycheck and helping someone else to make money, your million dollars is out there waiting for you to call to it. However, you are not heading towards it! You are doing nothing to bring the million dollars to you! Your current thinking, your thoughts, are stopping you from taking the action required to get you to your money. You are focusing on the worries and not the success. This type of thinking is an obstacle to your success.

It is possible to work on your path to a million dollars while having a separate full-time job, but it is more difficult. The path to a million dollars requires focused energy on your part. The more you can supply, the better the results you will have. At some point, you will need to focus 100% of your time on your million-dollar idea.

Coming up with a million-dollar idea can be done "on the side" while working at a full-time job. It is even possible that your full-time job will give you a million-dollar idea. Meanwhile, there are advantages to having money coming in from a full-time job, of course. However, at some point you will need more time to develop and work on your idea.

To prepare for this, save as much money as you can. There may be some "sacrifices" to be made, but they are investments in your future. Find every spare source of money and time available to you to give you the time and energy needed to focus on your million-dollar idea.

Some people's path to their million dollars starts with some introspection. Examine your thoughts and life. Then, decide if this "theft by paycheck" is a problem for you. If it is, decide how you will overcome it. There is a useful map in your hands as you read this, should you need it.

Theft by Critique

Some people worry what others will say about them if they announce they are starting a new project, a new business, or quitting a job to start something new. For many people, it is natural to worry about what other people will think about them or what other people say about them.

Many of the naysayers are secretly worried that you will succeed, thus proving that they failed (relatively) by not taking the actions to be successful as you did. So, your worries about what other people will think and say about you stem from unsuccessful people. Your thoughts about critique, which are holding you back from starting on your path to a million dollars, are coming from unsuccessful people! This type of thinking is another obstacle that is simply a thought—so control your thoughts.

Take it from your author and other millionaires in the world: focus on success. Take inspiration from successful people. (See HowToMakeaMillion.com if you need additional inspiration from successful people.) The people who have achieved what you want to achieve are the ones whose words you should let influence you, not those that want to hold you back.

Successful people often report that they were laughed at or critiqued in various ways prior to becoming successful. The reasons for this are not important, nor are the critiques. Whether it is having a book rejected many times before being published and achieving huge financial success (Harry Potter), having people flat out say a project will not work (GPS tour guide), being laughed at (Pet Rock), or any of the hundreds of other possible forms of criticism, having a strong desire to succeed mixed with a great idea you know will work will propel you past any worries about criticism. Again, you have a guidebook in your hands to assist you.

Further Down the Road

Theft by Paycheck and Theft by Critique are mentioned in this book because they are common issues in the minds of people who have not fully begun their acquisition of a million dollars. These initial "thought obstacles" are simply thoughts in your head.

There are two ways to banish these thoughts. The first is to train yourself to redirect your thoughts to positive thoughts when necessary. The second way is to come up with a million-dollar idea that fills you with desire and passion for it. The best solution is to do both of these things. Once you have your million-dollar idea, these obstacles disappear. Your belief in your idea and your passion for it will push you down the pathway to your money.

The pathway is clear:

First, you control your thoughts and get comfortable with money. Next, you focus on coming up with your million-dollar idea. For this, your reward is a great idea that is appropriate for you. After that, you focus on developing your plan and executing it. Executing your plan requires focus, which helps keep your thoughts controlled and positive.

Through all of this, it is your thoughts, which you control, that will lead you to success. In case you missed this, it is your thoughts, *which you control*, that will lead you to success.

Anything is Possible
(The Pet Rock Story)

All wealth is originally created in the manner described in this book. There are countless stories from our country's history that show the philosophy in this book is true.

It is possible to amass a fortune creating and selling new computers, selling hamburgers, creating a high-tech tour guide, creating and selling a new magazine, selling shoes from Argentina, sending out "What to do in NYC" emails, and countless other ways. It is even possible to make a million dollars selling small rocks.

What follows is the story about a man who did just that. Pay attention to the various elements of the following story. If you have read this book carefully and faithfully, you will recognize many tenets of this book's philosophy in the story.

A Man Sells Rocks

In the 1970s, Gary Dahl worked at an advertising agency in California. He spent his days thinking about how to help his clients market their products and services. He was a good copywriter and package designer. In the course of his work he learned that sometimes clever packaging is more important than the product itself.

One evening while in a bar with friends, the conversation turned to the topic of pets. His friends discussed the problems they had with their dogs and cats. The advertising man said that he had the perfect pet. He quipped, "I have a pet rock."

The jokes started immediately. The *San Jose Mercury News* later reported that he said his pet has "no vet bills, except once in a while to scrape off the moss..." The jokes continued. "It got hysterically funny," said Dahl. "No one took it seriously at all."

However, Dahl thought the idea of a pet rock was great. After spending his time focused on how to sell other people's products, he now had a brilliant idea for one of his own. The Universe delivered to him a great idea—and because of his background and experience he was the perfect person to make it happen.

Faith and Passion

Dahl reported that he developed a "passion" for his idea. "I believed in it," he said. His excitement for the idea and his belief led him to a local garden store where he purchased some stones for one penny each.

He used his package design talents to produce a special package for the rock—a cardboard Pet Rock carrying case, complete with air holes so the Pet Rock could breathe. A humorous instruction manual (Visit HowToMakeaMillion.

com for a link to see the actual manual) showed how to care for the pet. It explained it was easy to train your rock to "sit" and "stay." "Roll over" took a little assistance from the owner. Unfortunately, the Pet Rock was not very good at playing "fetch."

Timing

It is possible that the success of the Pet Rock was in part due to its timing. The country was just coming off two national problems—the war in Vietnam and the political scandal known as "Watergate." These national news events had put people in a poor mood. Everybody needed a little levity and humor, and it was about to be provided by the cute Pet Rock.

Marketing

The debut of Dahl's product came at a San Francisco gift show. Neiman Marcus placed an order for hundreds of the Pet Rocks. New York's Bloomingdale's store soon did the same. After the initial orders, Dahl put out a press release announcing the product and mentioned the existing sales. *Newsweek* magazine ran a story—and from there coverage of the Pet Rock exploded. Hundreds of newspapers covered the "story." Fancy department stores across the country clamored to stock and sell the Pet Rock.

The product was featured on television on the *Tonight Show* and Dahl was asked to be a guest on Johnny Carson's program. The fad of owning a Pet Rock swept the country and spawned knock-off products, add-on products, and even songs.

Within months, Dahl had his one million dollars. He became a millionaire by selling rocks that cost him one penny.

Review

This story is about an icon in American pop culture, but elements of the story occur in every wealth-building episode in the United States. Since this book is titled *How to Make a Million Dollars,* let's review the Pet Rock story to see how parts of it match topics covered in this book.

Prior to having his million-dollar idea, Gary Dahl *learned* about marketing. He knew how to design packages and use them to sell products.

Next, Gary Dahl had a fun *idea* in which he *believed.* Certainly, the idea of selling rocks is preposterous, but Dahl *decided* to pursue the opportunity anyway. He said he knew he was ready for success. He said he had to "take the plunge"—which meant that he understood the risks and worry. He took action anyway, based on his desire and passion. As we have learned, an idea mixed with *desire* and *faith* is a strong force.

Dahl's thoughts were not just that it was a funny idea to laugh about with his friends. He thought and believed that the idea was good and that people would buy a Pet Rock as a humorous novelty item. He "knew" it to be true and said himself that he developed a "*passion*" for it.

People *laughed at* his idea. They said *it would never work.* Despite them, he made it work. Dahl developed a *plan* and *took action.* He developed the product and for his initial marketing took it to a trade show. (Note: this might sound familiar as you recall the author took his GPS tour guide to a tourism trade show in New York City.) At the show, Dahl made his first sales. He *trademarked* his idea, which protected his name for the product, the Pet Rock.

His initial sales encouraged him. He began to *think big.* He took steps to further *market* his product. He produced a *press release* which garnered him worldwide exposure. The publicity generated so many sales that he shipped over one million rocks in four months.

In the course of this project, Dahl *"connected the dots"* from his life and utilized his strengths. He used his copy writing skills to develop the manual for the Pet Rock and his package design skills to produce the container for the rock.

Finally, in this age where so much attention is paid to men who make money using technology, it is interesting to note that Dahl used virtually no technology. He sold a rock.

You Are Ready

According to the *San Jose Mercury News*, Dahl reported: *"There's all that and then there's the fact that I believed in it. You have to have the passion to do it. You have to be ready to succeed, to take the giant leap. I was ready."*

As we discussed earlier, in order to make your million dollars, you must act. You must do something, but first *you have to be ready to succeed*. Dahl knew he was ready, and he decided to act.

The entirety of this book, including the Pet Rock story, is provided to help you acquire your million dollars (or more) should you decide to do so. This book exists to help you succeed.

When you are ready to succeed, a type of road map has been provided to you. Follow the path and philosophy in your own manner. You will be on your way to your million dollars.

Bonus: The Greatest Country in the World

———◆———

If you live in the United States of America, you live in the greatest country in the history of the world. There is more wealth, technology, and infrastructure in place, creating more opportunity than has existed anytime, anywhere.

There is more stored wealth in the country than in any other country in history. This means there is more for you to have and tap into than at any other time or place in the history of man. More wealth also means more opportunity, as people with money look for places to spend or invest their money.

How did this happen? What is it about the United States that makes it so full of opportunity? There is more than one causal factor, but the foundation of the country put in place at its genesis is one main reason.

"We hold these truths to be self-evident, that all men are created equal, that they are endowed by their Creator with certain unalienable Rights, that among these are Life, Liberty and the pursuit of Happiness," says the beginning of the Declaration of Independence.

The power, energy, and rights that you have in this country come from the Creator of man. This is not a book on religion, but it is important in your quest for a million dollars that you understand there is power that exists that is bigger than you are. The men who risked their lives when they signed the Declaration of Independence knew of this power. They also *decided* to create something new and beneficial to everyone on the continent of the "new world" of America. They based the country on this power.

The power does not come from the king or the government. The power is endowed by the Creator. All men in this country are equal in this very important aspect of life. This historic decision made by the country's founders is the basis of the success of the United States of America. History is full of men who had too much power and ruled against or used the people. This country is an attempt to keep the power in the hands of the people. What each person does with their power is up to them. (This means what *you* do with your power is up to *you*.)

After signing their own possible death sentences, the men who started this country made a plan to protect and defend their land. Just eleven years later, they mapped out another plan for a new government for their country. They wrote the U.S. Constitution. This carefully planned document is still the basis for the government of the country that has seen the most success of any country ever on the planet.

The power and energy on which this country is based is available to everyone. A poor black boy from Arkansas (John Johnson) used it to make hundreds of millions of dollars. A Buddhism-following college dropout (Steve Jobs) used it to make billions.

Still known as the "Land of Opportunity," almost one million people immigrate to the United States *each year*. The word is out that the U.S.A. is a good place to be—so much so that some people risk their lives to enter the country illegally.

Compare

Let us examine the United States and compare it to some other well-known countries to see where there is more opportunity:

The United States has less business regulation and lower tax rates than the restrictive socialist country of France. Taxes as a percent of Gross Domestic Product (GDP) (which is the total value of products and services produced in the country) are 45% in France versus 27% in the United States. Fewer restrictions and regulations make it much easier to start and run a successful business. Lower taxes mean you get to keep more of your own money, which gets you more quickly to your million dollars.

Eastern European countries are still shaking off the devastating impact of communist rule after World War II. In the thirty years since the Soviets left, the countries have made progress, but low wages and fewer opportunities are remnants of the ruined economy caused and left by the Soviets.

Communist China has made some advances for their people, but the country is not a "go to" place for opportunity. Historically, China has provided workers for projects in other countries. The mass manufacturing of the last decades is providing some opportunities, but they are very low-paying jobs.

Therefore, Western Europe, Eastern Europe, and the gigantic country of China do not provide good opportunities relative to those in the United States. These locations certainly do not have the best opportunities for those pursuing a million dollars.

Meanwhile in South America, socialism is crushing citizens' dreams and hopes. The people of Venezuela and Brazil have lived under corrupt systems for years. Mexico is so wonderful that hundreds of thousands of people literally walk out of the country each year.

While it is possible to be successful anywhere in the world, the United States of America still is the best "Land of Opportunity." Nowhere else on earth is there more opportunity. Freedom and resources are available to anyone who wants to tap into them.

What Do We Have?

We have a vast store of wealth, thanks to the hard work of those who have worked before us in our country. This wealth is easily seen in the gleaming skyscrapers of NYC, Los Angeles, San Francisco, Chicago, Dallas, Boston, etc. It is seen in the coast-to-coast Interstate highway system, which allows travel from sea-to-shining-sea without a fee or toll collected.

We have the ability to drive or fly coast-to-coast and speak the same language to everyone.

We have enough food, water, and entertainment to keep us fat, dumb, and happy if we wish.

We have libraries in every town in which knowledge and entertainment can be had for free.

We have the ability to use the Internet to research almost any topic from the comfort of a chair in our house. If we cannot afford Internet, the local library will provide it for free.

We have grocery stores that have full shelves of food from all over the world, including multiple sources of bottled water should you decide the water from the tap that your municipality provides is not to your liking.

We have the ability to have something shipped on a Thursday in Australia show up on our doorstep on the other side of the planet, in the U.S.A., on Monday.

We have eradicated many diseases that used to cause death. Life expectancies have increased.

We have stored wealth handed from one generation to the next. In some cases, the wealth is used to fund health research. In some cases, it is used to fund public art. In some cases, it is used to fund other capitalistic endeavors (i.e., start businesses and create more wealth and more benefit to other people).

We have people who give their stored wealth to colleges and universities so other people can learn and have better lives.

We have people whose stored wealth is given as scholarships to students so they can learn and have better lives.

We have entertainment of so many types there is no time to watch, read, or listen to all of it.

Travel that used to take days or weeks by wagon or automobile is now accomplished in hours via airplane.

With the push of a button, we can summon a car with a driver to pick us up and take us wherever we choose.

We have the world's best inventors and innovators in Silicon Valley. We have some of the world's best movies made in Hollywood. We have amazing television programs and Broadway shows made in New York City, all of which bring in millions of dollars *each week*. We have amazing agricultural advances coming from the Midwest of the country.

We have the best hospitals in the world, with patients flying in from around the globe to receive the best treatment possible.

We can talk on the telephone or computer to anyone anywhere in the world and include a live video feed. The cost is almost nothing!

We have free distribution of information via websites, including text, photos, and videos.

We have the ability to publish a book using technology found in most people's homes and have copies of the book delivered to our front doorsteps (or anywhere else in the world).

We have the ability to communicate with strangers in a location that we intend to visit and ask them questions about their town/city/location.

We have freedom of religion: the country was founded on Christianity, but everyone is free to worship as he wishes. Steve Jobs (Apple Computer) practiced Buddhism. Sergey Brin (Google) is Jewish.

Business owners can use computers and software to save time and decrease costs—including in the tedious areas of bookkeeping, invoicing, and payroll. "Bookkeeping" used to require a book. Now everything is saved electronically, and computers do calculations formerly done by hand.

Payment can be made online from anyone, anywhere in the world, in any currency, and it is easily converted to U.S. dollars.

The computing power used to put a man on the moon (another American achievement) is now available to anyone—on their handheld phone!

A Good Time and Place

With freedom from too much business regulation, advances in communication, advances in technology, and the power on which this country was built, there has never been a better time or place on earth to tap into the available resources and ask for whatever you wish. There has never been a better time to make a million dollars (or much more!) than now.

Opportunities exist for whomever wishes to follow the steps of the process that takes you to your desired wealth. These steps are part of Nature. The power and energy are available to everyone, everywhere, but especially in the United States of America. So do it.

Good luck to you.

CPSIA information can be obtained
at www.ICGtesting.com
Printed in the USA
BVHW041146210621
610128BV00009B/132/J